PRESIDENTIAL IMPEACHMENT

AN AMERICAN DILEMMA

CONSULTING EDITOR

James Neal Primm
University of Missouri-St. Louis

PRESIDENTIAL IMPEACHMENT

AN AMERICAN DILEMMA

WALTER EHRLICH

University of Missouri — St. Louis

With an introduction by
RICHARD DUDMAN
CHIEF WASHINGTON CORRESPONDENT
ST. LOUIS POST-DISPATCH

FORUM PRESS

Published simultaneously in Canada.

Printed in the United States of America.

Library of Congress Catalog Card Number: 73-92315

ISBN: 0-88273-104-1

First Printing April 1974
Second Printing May 1974

Cover Design by Daniel Pearlmutter

To Sylvia

Preface

On July 31, 1973, Congressman Robert F. Drinan of Massachusetts introduced the following resolution in the House of Representatives: "Resolved, That Richard M. Nixon, President of the United States, is impeached of high crimes and misdemeanors." An American dilemma, the possibility of a presidential impeachment, had become a stark reality.

The word "impeachment" carries a somber and frightening ring for most Americans. For the past century, especially since the impeachment and trial of President Andrew Johnson in 1868, suggestions that this constitutional remedy be applied to check executive abuses and encroachments have been considered unthinkable, almost heretical. Impeachment is a grave, awesome matter, charging a public official with misconduct serious enough to warrant his removal from office. Yet many misconceptions abound regarding what impeachment really is. Perhaps the greatest is its connotation of something so fearful, so unthinkable. The Founding Fathers placed this procedure in the Constitution because they realistically foresaw the necessity to remove abusive and corrupt officials. They saw impeachment not as something to fear, but rather as a legitimate means to protect against abuse and tyranny, to be used prudently, but to be used whenever needed.

The term "impeachment" itself is often misused. Impeachment is only the first of two steps necessary for removal from office. A comparable process is the criminal proceeding of indictment and trial. Indictment is a formal accusation by a grand jury. It does not mean that the accused is guilty; it indicates only that there is sufficient evidence to justify a trial. The second step, the trial, occurs before the petit jury, and only there can the accused by found guilty. Procedurally, impeachment is comparable with a grand jury indictment. It is a formal accusation by the House of Representatives that an official may have committed an act or acts justifying removal. If impeached by the House, the official is then tried in the Senate, and only there can he be found guilty, or "convicted." The term "impeachment" is often erroneously used to describe the entire process. One often hears, for instance, that no President has ever been impeached. President Andrew Johnson *was* impeached; he was not *convicted*.

Another misconception involves the nature of impeachment. Because it is commonly equated with criminal indictment, impeachment is assumed by many to be a criminal procedure too. This is incorrect. Impeachment (and subsequent trial) is not a judicial action. It is a political decision (a vote) made by a political institution (the elected members of Congress) to remove a political official (the President, Vice-President, or other civil officers of the United States). Indeed, the only "punishment" allowed by the Constitution is removal from office. If the misdeed happens to be a criminal act, once the official is out of office he may be dealt with as an ordinary citizen in an appropriate criminal procedure.

Still another widespread misconception involves grounds for impeachment. Because many incorrectly conceive impeachment as a criminal procedure, they equally incorrectly assume that an official can be impeached only for an indictable criminal offense. The result has been that non-criminal but still impeachable political abuses of public office have been overlooked for lack of indictable criminality. Knowledge of the history and development of impeachment will correct this misconception.

The purpose of this volume is to examine that history and development by interpretive essay and supportive documentary materials. One important source of information is *Impeachment — Selected Materials*, House Committee Print, Committee on the Judiciary, House of Representatives, 93rd Congress, 1st Session, October, 1973 (Washington, D.C., 1973). Another is the outstanding scholarly study of English legal precedents in Raoul Berger, *Impeachment: The Constitutional Problems* (Cambridge, 1973).

I want to express my deepest thanks to Professor James Neal Primm of the University of Missouri-St. Louis and to the editor of Forum Press, Daniel Sortwell, for invaluable reading and editorial assistance, and to Judith Thomasson for diligent proof-reading. My thanks to George H. Hall of the *St. Louis Post-Dispatch* for permission to reprint materials from that newspaper. For their most constructive observations about impeachment and impeachability, my profoundest appreciation to Professors Raoul Berger and Archibald Cox of the Harvard Law School and to Thomas B. Curtis, former Congressman from Missouri. Above all, I want to thank my family for tolerating me and my idiosyncracies during the writing of this book.

St. Louis, Missouri   *WALTER EHRLICH*

Contents

Introduction

By the start of 1974 it seemed that the Watergate scandal had reached the point where Richard M. Nixon would soon quit the Presidency one way or another. Evidence of payoff, deception and cover-up had far overshadowed the original burglary at Democratic Party headquarters. Polls and surveys and soundings by vacationing Congressmen showed that most Americans no longer trusted President Nixon. Yet what to do about it puzzled them deeply.

Resignation, it seemed to many, would clear the air and restore normal government, especially after a decent and honest Vice-President was in place and ready to take over. But Mr. Nixon, combative as ever, showed no sign that he would step down voluntarily.

Impeachment, however, remained frightening and unfamiliar ground. To many it seemed unfair, almost regardless of the provocation, an abridgement of the traditional right of every individual to be presumed innocent until convicted of a crime. A prominent California Democratic politician visiting in Washington showed the common misunderstanding of the impeachment process; he told newsmen he considered impeachment to be improper until the President had been proven guilty. He had forgotten, if he ever knew, that impeachment is the *bringing* of charges by the House of Representatives, whereas the trial is conducted by the Senate.

It had been more than a century since a President was impeached, and that lone example was generally thought to have been a catastrophic failure because it grew out of partisan politics. Even the impeachment of a lesser official had not been achieved for some 38 years.

Deep in the national subconscious, too, impeachment seemed to arouse the same dreads and anxieties as Presidential assassination or regicide. Some Freudian psychiatrists argued that in the recesses of the mind impeachment was related to patricide, a son's murder of his father, with the son's accompanying fear of failure and retaliatory castration.

Whatever the reasons, the impeachment process was widely feared and misunderstood. A course in public education was in order. Part of that course would come as the process itself went forward. The House of Representatives crossed the Rubicon when it voted one million dollars for an investigation by the Judiciary Committee to determine whether an impeachment resolution should be brought to the House floor. With the selection of special counsel and the creation of a special staff, the machinery began to grind in earnest, although so unobtrusively that the public was hardly aware of it at first. The House, however, was already committed to a proceeding that would lead to a vote in the committee; if that carried, to a vote on the House floor, and, if impeachment was voted, to a trial before the Senate. Each step would be a stage in public education, a part of a process of getting used to the idea of using the mechanism provided by the Constitution for getting rid of a President deemed to have disqualified himself.

By late winter, the tempo had quickened. A series of upset Democratic victories in special Congressional elections showed Democrats that attacking the President was a winning issue and persuaded many Republicans that he would be a millstone around their necks if he remained in office by the November elections. The spectacle of former top White House associates facing criminal prosecution gave further impetus to the idea of impeachment. At the same time, the President, who had promised to "fight like hell," counterattacked against his critics, withheld evidence from the impeachment inquiry, and through a small army of defense lawyers tried to force the Judiciary Committee to narrow its investigation and its definition of an impeachable offense.

There could be little doubt that the country was in for a bitter, bruising, polarizing fight, probably worse than anything experienced since the Civil War and yet a constitutional necessity to resolve the nation's worst scandal.

At each stage of this process, unexplored in the lifetime or memory of any living American, there must be informed public debate. And that is where this book comes in. Professor Ehrlich is supplying the information and analysis that can help Americans understand the impeachment process without fear and work their way out of the worst government crisis in at least a century and possibly in the nation's entire 200-year history.

Richard Dudman
Chief Washington Correspondent
St. Louis Post-Dispatch

1
Origins of Impeachment

THE ROOTS of impeachment lie in fourteenth-century England, weakened by partisan struggles of baronial factions, by heavy taxation, and by the military drains of the Hundred Years' War. During this period the representative element of Parliament, soon to be known as the House of Commons, began to acquire the power of the purse. When the king asked for money, especially for military purposes, Commons made the grant dependent upon the remedy of grievances, either for itself as a part of Parliament or for the classes it represented. Gradually Parliament increased its role in legislation, in taxation, and even in occasional efforts to control executive policy. With this increasing power, Parliament was able to legislate the Statute of Treasons in 1352, defining more clearly the roles of the older royal courts and the newly emerging Parliament in dealing with abusive and corrupt officials. In 1376, in an action that previously would have been a royal court prerogative, two of King Edward III's foremost ministers, Lord Latimer and Lord Lyons, were accused by the Commons of malversation and war profiteering. They were convicted by the Lords, removed from office, fined, and imprisoned. A few years later, Chancellor Michael de la Pole, the Earl of Suffolk, was accused of the "high crime and misdemeanor" of using appropriated funds for purposes other than those specified, but he fled before the Lords could try him. These actions were grounded primarily on the legal maxim that while the King could do no wrong, his ministers were responsible for their own acts. The form of the actions was "impeachment," derived from the Latin *impedicare*, meaning "to hinder" or "to prevent"; in parliamentary usage it meant "accusation" or "charge." The procedure was accusation by the Commons and trial in the Lords.

A number of impeachment proceedings were brought during the late fourteenth and early fifteenth centuries, but following the impeachment and conviction of the Duke of Suffolk in 1450 (for procuring offices for persons unfit and unworthy of them), the procedure fell into disuse for more than a century. This was due partly to the instability of Parliament during the Wars of the Roses, and in part to the unique relationship between Crown and Parliament during the Tudor period, 1485-1603. England was embroiled in crucial domestic and foreign problems involving the succession to the throne, the Reformation, and the emergence of England as a major European power. It was the turbulent era of Henry VIII and Elizabeth, of "Bloody Mary" Tudor and Mary Stuart, of Sir Francis Drake and the Spanish Armada. Rather than risk internal strife by attempting to check abusive royal ministers, Parliament increasingly acceded to Tudor prerogatives to ensure the eventual safety and security of England. Thus powerful Tudor monarchs were able to coerce Parliament into accepting certain ministerial actions, and into sanctioning royal dismissals and condemnations through bills of attainder (quasi-judicial sentences or punishments decreed by a legislature rather than by a court). Ministers seemed completely creatures of the Crown, with Parliament a malleable instrument of royal enforcement.

With the accession of James I, first of the Stuarts, in 1603, the stage was set for a constitutional confrontation between Crown and Parliament. Many achievements of the Tudors became encumbrances for the Stuarts. There was no longer danger from a disputed succession, dissident nobles had been suppressed, the Reformation issues appeared settled, and the British Isles no longer were threatened by foreign invasion. England was peaceful and prosperous, and many felt that the safeguard of a strong monarchy was no longer essential. Toward the end of Elizabeth's reign Parliament already showed a disposition to oppose the royal will, but loyalty to the aged queen, last of the direct descendants of Henry VIII, prevailed. When James I, Elizabeth's Scottish cousin, advanced the theory of divine right — that the monarch was responsible neither to Parliament nor to the nation — Parliament was convinced that the time had come to retrieve its lost powers.

James's unpopular and repressive policies precipitated and exacerbated the confrontation. Conflicts developed over seemingly settled religious issues, over the union with Scotland, over finances, over the jurisdiction of various judges and courts, over foreign involvements, and especially over the extent of royal authority *vis-a-vis* Parliament. By the time Charles I succeeded his father in 1625, Parliament was ready to oppose any and all claims of the Crown to supremacy.

In challenging royal authority, Parliament recognized that confrontation risked the necessity of enforcing laws of treason to their fullest extent, even if it meant the execution of the King. Because at first this extreme was virtually unthinkable, they refrained from a direct assault on the King. Instead, they revived the common law theorem that while the King could do no wrong his ministers were culpable. In a series of crucial and momentous prosecutions, Parliament resurrected the impeachment weapon and challenged a number of oppressive and highhanded ministers for "high crimes and misdemeanors." Among those impeached and removed were Lord Treasurer Middlesex (in 1624, for corruption in accepting gifts and for misusing appropriated funds), the Duke of Buckingham (in 1626, for nepotism and for failing "as a great admiral to safeguard the seas," abetted no doubt by the intense hatred toward him because of his strong affection for Catholic France and Spain), Justice Robert Berkeley (in 1637, for threatening a grand jury and other abusive action on the bench), and Sir Richard Gurney, Lord Mayor of London (in 1642, for interfering with a directive of Parliament dealing with the storage of arms and ammunition). Perhaps the most significant was the impeachment and conviction of the Earl of Strafford in 1642 for "subverting the fundamental law and introducing arbitrary and tyrannical government." The result was the removal of a number of key ministers of Stuart absolutism and the re-establishment of Parliamentary authority. Perhaps at no other time in England's history did a legal weapon, impeachment, achieve such momentous victories over tyranny. Still the King persisted. Stripped of most of his capable advisers and many of his powers, Charles I nevertheless pressed his design for royal supremacy. It brought on the tragic civil wars of the 1640's and led inexorably to his fateful rendezvous in 1649 with the executioner's axe.

Divisive internal struggles in the Cromwellian and Restoration periods soon subverted the role of impeachment. What had been the principal legal weapon to combat royal tyranny gradually evolved into an instrument of party and factional struggles, a device to attack unpopular political opponents and policies. The removal of the Earl of Strafford in 1642 had been aimed unquestionably at the arbitrariness and absolutism of the Crown. It was the last impeachment clearly for this purpose. Once Parliament gained ascendancy, and especially after the Glorious Revolution of 1688 and the English Bill of Rights of 1689, royal absolutist aspirations were replaced by other internal political problems, and the role of impeachment accordingly changed. Proceedings against the Earl of Arlington (1674), Chief Justice William Scroggs (1680), the Duke of Leeds (1695), the Earl of Orford (1701), Viscount Bolingbroke (1715), and the Earl of Oxford (1717) reflect a changing view toward "high crimes and misdemeanors." Neither offenses nor ministers were associated with royal absolutism that would challenge Parliament's rights and prerogatives. Instead they represented corruption, or the advocacy of unwise or unpopular policies, or inability to provide the leadership that Parliament deemed necessary for the security of the nation.

During the reigns of the Hanoverians George I and George II, the supremacy of Parliament over the Crown was firmly established. This was due partly to the victory of constitutionalism over absolutism during the Stuart era; it was due partly to the first two Hanoverians being more German than English and relinquishing and virtually abdicating many of their powers to Parliament and the ministers; it was due partly to the achievements of Sir Robert Walpole, England's first great prime minister, in establishing a new and vital role for the prime minister and the cabinet. Part of this new role involved the status of the ministers. Nominally responsible to the Crown, more and more their accountability was to Parliament, just as other aspects of the government came under Parliament's control. Impeachment of oppressive officials became an unnecessary mechanism. Parliament no longer had to pressure the Crown to dismiss a miscreant minister; its own mere protestation became sufficient. By the time of George II, the instrument known as the "Address" to the King had appeared, a request by Parliament for the removal of a particularly undesirable minister. Gradually this evolved into the now familiar "vote of censure" and "vote of confidence" procedures associated with parliamentary government and became the major device to thwart abusive and corrupt officials. Impeachment was used less and less. It emerged occasionally during the eighteenth century, as in the trials of Lord Chancellor Macclesfield, Lord Lovat, and Warren Hastings, each a spectacular event, but primarily impeachment survived as the mechanism for removing corrupt and dishonest judges rather than political officials. This was the background of impeachment in England when the Constitutional Convention met in Philadelphia in 1787.

Impeachment was little used in colonial America. This is understandable since with few exceptions executive and judicial posts in the colonies were royal appointments made at the King's pleasure, terminable at his discretion. Thus in Pennsylvania, in 1706, when the colonial assembly brought impeachment charges against an agent of the proprietor, the governor refused to approve the procedure, asserting that only the English Parliament, and not a colonial assembly, had this power. On the other hand, the colonial council (but not the elected assembly) of North Carolina had the right to bring charges against its governor. One example occurred in the 1730's. Governor George Burrington was constantly at odds with the assembly, and on one occasion four members of his council sided with it. The governor promptly suspended the four councilors. In his report to the Board of Trade, Burrington referred to one as "an ungrateful villain altogether bent upon mischief," to the second as "a man of most infamous character," to the third as "a disgrace to the Council," and to the fourth, who incidentally was also chief justice of the colony, as "a silly rash boy, a busy fool and egregious sot, . . . an ungrateful perfidious scoundrel." The four councilors thereupon brought countercharges against Burrington, accusing him of "high misdemeanors." The Board of Trade upheld the councilors and removed the governor from office. This was a rare instance of removal, and the final action came by the Board of Trade in London rather than by the colonial legislature. In general, rather than impeachment, the primary weapon employed in the colonies to check arbitrary officials was the control by the legislature over taxation, the "power of the purse." Time after time a colonial governor was prevented from carrying out unpopular measures by the assembly's refusal to appropriate funds. In some colonies the governor's salary was withheld until he acceded to the legislature. The history of how colonial legislatures were able to keep a check on colonial governors by the power of the purse is well recorded.

When the colonies declared their independence in 1776, sovereignty moved to this side of the Atlantic. New state constitutions were drafted (Connecticut and Rhode Island merely extended their colonial charters), and all contained some form of removal of abusive governmental officials. Some constitutions provided for procedures similar to the "Address" in England, some for impeachment. Some stated specific grounds for removal, others used such vague terms as "misbehavior" or "maladministration." Some stipulated that the removal proceeding could lead to a civil prosecution, and some limited such follow-up litigations to criminal cases. Although they differed in how it was to be implemented, every state constitution contained the principle that circumstances might necessitate the forced removal of erring officials. The following impeachment provision in the Virginia constitution of 1776 illustrates this principle:

The Governour . . . and others offending against the State, either by Mal-administration, Corruption, or other Means, by which the safety of the State may be endangered, shall be impeachable by the House of Delegates. Such impeachment to be prosecuted by the Attorney General, or such other Person or Persons as the House may appoint in the General Court, according to the laws of the Land. If found guilty, he or they shall be either for ever disabled to hold any Office under Government, or removed from such Office *Pro tempore*, or subjected to such Pains or Penalties as the laws shall direct.

If all, or any of the Judges of the General Court, should, on good grounds (to be judged of by the House of Delegates) be accused of any of the Crimes or Offences beforementioned, such House of Delegates may, in like manner, impeach the Judge or Judges so accused, to be prosecuted in the Court of Appeals; and he or they, if found guilty, shall be punished in the same manner as is prescribed in the preceding Clause.

The delegates to the Constitutional Convention in 1787 were well informed about the history of impeachment in England. "The shades of despotic kings and conniving ministers marched before them," writes Professor Raoul Berger. A genuine concern at Philadelphia was the gnawing fear that the new chief executive might become a Stuart-type monarch, one who could destroy their aspirations for the new American state. But the delegates' knowledge of and their own experience with colonial government, and briefly with state government, convinced them that the current English method of combatting governmental abuses — the system of cabinet accountability and the vote of confidence — would not meet their purposes. The Founding Fathers wanted a strong executive, but they also wanted a limited executive, independent but accountable for its acts. To achieve this, they imaginatively fashioned England's impeachment process to fit the American experiment in separation of powers. Out of their deliberations was to come the Constitutional provision: "The President, Vice-President, and all civil Officers of the United States shall be removed from Office on Impeachment for, and Conviction of, Treason, Bribery, or other high Crimes and Misdemeanors."

That wording was not arrived at casually. Impeachment, treason, bribery, high crimes and misdemeanors were terms taken directly from English law. To understand what they meant to the Framers, it is necessary to trace the evolution of the terminology in the discussions at the Constitutional Convention. James Madison's Journal makes this possible.

Shortly after the Convention opened, Edmund Randolph submitted the Virginia Plan (the brainchild of James Madison, "father of the Constitution"), which contained the basic principles and general form of government that eventually emerged. It called for a national executive, a national legislature, and a national judiciary, part of which would be a supreme court with authority over "impeachments of any National officers."

TUESDAY, MAY 29, IN CONVENTION

Resolutions proposed by Mr. Randolph . . .

7. Resolved that a National Executive be instituted; to be chosen by the National Legislature for the term of years, . . . and to be ineligible a second time; . . .

9. Resolved that a National Judiciary be established to consist of one or more supreme tribunals, and of inferior

tribunals to be chosen by the National Legislature, to hold their offices during good behaviour; . . . that the jurisdiction of the inferior tribunals shall be to hear and determine in the first instance, and of the supreme tribunal to hear and determine in the dernier resort, . . . impeachments of any National officers, and questions which may involve the national peace and harmony. . . .

Serious disagreements developed over the chief executive's term of office and eligibility for re-election. A long term might allow him to become too independent, even a tyrant if unchecked. Fears of a Stuart-type despotism were frequently expressed. Furthermore, what if the executive became incapacitated? An impeachment, argued Gunning Bedford of Delaware, would reach "misfeasance" only, not incapacity. This vague terminology was beclouded even more when George Mason argued for the necessity of removing an "unfit" official. "Unfit" was shortly defined when it was agreed that the executive should be removable "on impeachment and conviction of mal-practice or neglect of duty."

FRIDAY JUNE 1, 1787

The Committee of the whole proceeded to Resolution 7. "that a national Executive be instituted, to be chosen by the national Legislature — for the term of   years and to be ineligible thereafter, to possess the executive powers of Congress."

Mr. PINKNEY was for a vigorous Executive but was afraid the Executive powers of the existing Congress might extend to peace and war, which would render the Executive a monarchy, of the worst kind, to wit an elective one.

Mr. WILSON moved that the Executive consist of a single person.

Mr. C. PINKNEY seconded the motion, so as to read "that a National Executive to consist of a single person, be instituted. . . ."

The next clause in Resolution 7, relating to the mode of appointing, and the duration of, the Executive being under consideration,

Mr. WILSON said he was almost unwilling to declare the mode which he wished to take place, being apprehensive that it might appear chimerical. He would say however at least that in theory he was for an election by the people. . . .

Mr. WILSON moved that the blank for the term of

duration should be filled with three years, observing at the same time that he preferred this short period, on the supposition that a re-eligibility would be provided for.

Mr. PINKNEY moved for seven years.

Mr. SHERMAN was for three years, and against the doctrine of rotation as throwing out of office the men best qualifyed to execute its duties.

Mr. MASON was for seven years at least, and for prohibiting a re-eligibility as the best expedient both for preventing the effect of a false complaisance on the side of the Legislature towards unfit characters; and a temptation on the side of the Executive to intrigue with the Legislature for a re-appointment.

Mr. BEDFORD was strongly opposed to so long a term as seven years. He begged the committee to consider what the situation of the Country would be, in case the first magistrate should be saddled on it for such a period and it should be found on trial that he did not possess the qualifications ascribed to him, or should lose them after his appointment. An impeachment he said would be no cure for this evil, as an impeachment would reach misfeasance only, not incapacity. He was for a triennial election, and for an ineligibility after a period of nine years.

On the question for seven years,

Mass. divided. Conn. no. N.Y. ay. N.J. ay. Penn. ay. Del. ay. Virg. ay. N.C. no. S.C. no. Geor. no. There being 5 ays, 4 noes, 1 divided, a question was asked whether a majority had voted in the affirmative? The President decided that it was an affirmative vote. . . .

SATURDAY, JUNE 2, 1787

Mr. DICKENSON moved "that the Executive be made removeable by the National Legislature on the request of a majority of the Legislatures of individual States." It was necessary he said to place the power of removing somewhere. He did not like the plan of impeaching the Great officers of State. He did not know how provision could be made for removal of them in a better mode than that which he had proposed. He had no idea of abolishing the State Governments as some gentlemen seemed inclined to do. The happiness of this Country in his opinion required considerable powers to be left in the hands of the States.

Mr. BEDFORD seconded the motion.

Mr. SHERMAN contended that the National Legislature should have power to remove the Executive at pleasure.

Mr. MASON. Some mode of displacing an unfit magistrate is rendered indispensable by the fallibility of those who choose, as well as by the corruptibility of the man chosen. He opposed decidedly the making the Executive the mere creature of the Legislature as a violation of the fundamental principle of good Government.

Mr. MADISON and Mr. WILSON observed that it would leave an equality of agency in the small with the great States; that it would enable a minority of the people to prevent the removal of an officer who had rendered himself justly criminal in the eyes of a majority; that it would open a door for intrigues against him in States where his administration though just might be unpopular, and might tempt him to pay court to particular States whose leading partizans he might fear, or wish to engage as his partizans. They both thought it bad policy to introduce such a mixture of the State authorities, where their agency could be otherwise supplied.

Mr. DICKENSON considered the business as so important that no man ought to be silent or reserved. He went into a discourse of some length, the sum of which was, that the Legislative, Executive, and Judiciary departments ought to be made as independent as possible; but that such an Executive as some seemed to have in contemplation was not consistent with a republic; that a firm Executive could only exist in a limited monarchy. . . .

A motion being made to strike out "on request by a majority of the Legislatures of the individual States" and rejected, Connecticut, S. Carol. and Geo. being ay, the rest no: the question was taken —

On Mr. DICKENSON'S motion for making Executive removeable by National Legislature at request of majority of State Legislatures was also rejected — all the States being in the negative Except Delaware which gave an affirmative vote.

The question for making the Executive ineligible after seven years was next taken, and agreed to:

Mass. ay. Conn. no. N.Y. ay. Pa. div. Del. ay. Md. ay. Virg. ay. N.C. ay. S.C. ay. Geo. no.

Mr. WILLIAMSON seconded by Mr. DAVIE moved to add to the last Clause, the words — "and to be removeable on impeachment and conviction of mal-practice or neglect of duty" — which was agreed to. . . .

WEDNESDAY, JUNE 13, IN COMMITTEE OF THE WHOLE

REPORT OF COMMITTEE OF WHOLE ON MR. RANDOLPH'S PROPOSITIONS

9. Resolved that a National Executive be instituted to consist of a single person, to be chosen by the National Legislature for the term of seven years, with power to carry

into execution the national laws, to appoint to offices in cases not otherwise provided for — to be ineligible a second time, and to be removeable on impeachment and conviction of malpractices or neglect of duty. . . .

11. Resolved that a National Judiciary be established, to consist of one supreme tribunal, the Judges of which to be appointed by the second branch of the National Legislature, to hold their offices during good behaviour, . . .

The Virginia Plan was a starter; other proposals soon followed. The New Jersey Plan, presented by the distinguished lawyer William Paterson, called for a national executive removable by Congress "on application by a majority of the Executives of the several States," but it did not state any grounds for such removal. The brilliant Alexander Hamilton of New York proposed a strong central government in which all the national officers would be subject to "impeachment for mal- and corrupt conduct," all impeachments to be tried by a special court consisting of the chief justices of each state.

FRIDAY, JUNE 15th

Mr. PATTERSON . . .

4. Resolved that the United States in Congress be authorized to elect a federal Executive to consist of   persons, to continue in office for the term of   years, . . . to be ineligible a second time, and removeable by Congress on application by a majority of the Executives of the several States; . . .

5. Resolved that a federal Judiciary be established to consist of a supreme Tribunal the Judges of which to be appointed by the Executive, and to hold their offices during good behaviour, . . . that the Judiciary so established shall have authority to hear and determine in the first instance on all impeachments of federal officers, . . .

MONDAY, JUNE 18, 1787

Mr. HAMILTON . . .

IX. The Governour, Senators and all officers of the United States to be liable to impeachment for mal- and corrupt conduct; and upon conviction to be removed from office, and disqualified for holding any place of trust or profit — All impeachments to be tried by a Court to consist of the Chief   or Judge of the superior Court of Law of each State, provided such Judge shall hold his place during good behavior, and have a permanent salary. . . .

On July 20 the delegates debated at length the impeachability of the chief executive. Charles Cotesworth Pinckney, a South Carolina planter and lawyer, opposed the impeachment provision; he feared for the independence of the executive, with the legislature holding impeachment "as a rod" over him. Peg-legged Gouverneur Morris originally opposed impeachment, but later conceded that corruption and other misdeeds might be impeachable as long as the offenses were clearly enumerated and defined. Strong arguments for impeachment were presented by George Mason, Benjamin Franklin, James Madison, Elbridge Gerry, and Edmund Randolph, all influential and highly respected delegates. The Convention finally voted, 8-2, that the executive should be impeachable, but delegates still disagreed on the details. Very revealing were the grounds justifying impeachment — corruption, misconduct, negligence, perfidy, treachery, misbehavior, perverting the administration into a scheme of peculation or oppression, corrupting his electors, betraying a trust to a foreign power. In light of later contentions that a President is impeachable only for indictable crimes, these arguments take on added significance. The Framers clearly referred to actions many of which were neither indictable nor criminal. There was no doubt that a criminal act was punishable and that impeachment and removal did not diminish the liability of a criminal offender to prosecution later in the regular courts. Indeed, the only reference to anything specifically "criminal" was George Mason's comment that when any "great crimes" were committed he favored "punishing the principal as well as the Coadjutors." What concerned the delegates was to make certain that impeachment would apply to non-criminal misconduct as well as to criminal.

FRIDAY, JULY 20. IN CONVENTION

"to be removeable on impeachment and conviction for malpractice or neglect of duty." see Resol: 9.

Mr. PINKNEY and Mr. Govr. MORRIS moved to strike out this part of the Resolution. Mr. P. observed he ought not to be impeachable whilst in office.

Mr. DAVIE. If he be not impeachable whilst in office, he will spare no efforts or means whatever to get himself re-elected. He considered this as an essential security for the good behaviour of the Executive.

Mr. WILSON concurred in the necessity of making the Executive impeachable whilst in office.

Mr. Govr. MORRIS. He can do no criminal act without Coadjutors who may be punished. In case he should be re-elected, that will be sufficient proof of his innocence. Besides who is to impeach? Is the impeachment to suspend his functions. If it is not the mischief will go on. If it is the impeachment will be nearly equivalent to a displacement, and will render the Executive dependent on those who are to impeach.

Col. MASON. No point is of more importance than that the right of impeachment should be continued. Shall any man be above Justice? Above all shall that man be above it, who can commit the most extensive injustice? When great crimes were committed he was for punishing the principal as well as the Coadjutors. There had been much debate and difficulty as to the mode of chusing the Executive. He approved of that which had been adopted at first, namely of referring the appointment to the National Legislature. One objection against Electors was the danger of their being corrupted by the Candidates; and this furnished a peculiar reason in favor of impeachments whilst in office. Shall the man who has practised corruption and by that means procured his appointment in the first instance, be suffered to escape punishment, by repeating his guilt?

Docr. FRANKLIN was for retaining the clause as favorable to the Executive. History furnishes one example only of a first Magistrate being formally brought to public Justice. Everybody cried out against this as unconstitutional. What was the practice before this in cases where the chief Magistrate rendered himself obnoxious? Why recourse was had to assassination in which he was not only deprived of his life but of the opportunity of vindicating his character. It would be the best way therefore to provide in the Constitution for the regular punishment of the Executive where his misconduct should deserve it, and for his honorable acquittal when he should be unjustly accused.

Mr. Govr. MORRIS admits corruption and some few other offences to be such as ought to be impeachable; but thought the cases ought to be enumerated and defined:

Mr. MADISON thought it indispensable that some provision should be made for defending the Community against the incapacity, negligence or perfidy of the chief Magistrate. The limitation of the period of his service, was not a sufficient security. He might lose his capacity after his appointment. He might pervert his administration into a scheme of peculation or oppression. He might betray his trust to foreign powers. The case of the Executive Magistracy was very distinguishable, from that of the Legislature or of any other public body, holding offices of limited duration. It could not be presumed that all or even a majority of the members of an Assembly would either lose their capacity for discharging, or be bribed to betray, their trust. Besides the restraints of their personal integrity and honor, the difficulty of acting in concert for purposes of corruption was a security to the public. And if one or a few members only should be seduced, the soundness of the remaining members, would maintain the integrity and fidelity of the body. In the case of the Executive Magistracy which was to be administered by a single man, loss of capacity or corruption was more within the compass of probable events, and either of them might be fatal to the Republic.

Mr. PINKNEY did not see the necessity of impeachments. He was sure they ought not to issue from the Legislature who would in that case hold them as a rod over the Executive and by that means effectually destroy his independence. His revisionary power in particular would be rendered altogether insignificant.

Mr. GERRY urged the necessity of impeachments. A good magistrate will not fear them. A bad one ought to be kept in fear of them. He hoped the maxim would never be adopted here that the chief magistrate could do no wrong.

Mr. KING expressed his apprehensions that an extreme caution in favor of liberty might enervate the Government we were forming. He wished the House to recur to the primitive axiom that the three great departments of Government should be separate and independent; that the Executive and Judiciary should be so as well as the Legislative; that the Executive should be so equally with the Judiciary. Would this be the case, if the Executive should be impeachable? It had been said that the Judiciary would be impeachable. But it should have been remembered at the same time that the Judiciary hold their places not for a limited time, but during good behaviour. It is necessary therefore that a forum should be established for trying misbehaviour. Was the Executive to hold his place during good behaviour? The Executive was to hold his place for a limited term like the members of the Legislature: Like them particularly the Senate whose members would continue in appointment the same term of 6 years he would periodically be tried for his behaviour by his electors, who would continue or discontinue him in trust according to the manner in which he had discharged it. Like them therefore, he ought to be subject to no intermediate trial, by impeachment. He ought not to be impeachable unless he held his office during good behaviour, a tenure which would be most agreeable to him; provided an independent and effectual forum could be devised. But under no circumstances ought he to be impeachable by the Legislature. This would be destructive of his independence and of the principles of the Constitution. He relied on the vigor of the Executive as a great security for the public liberties.

Mr. RANDOLPH. The propriety of impeachments was a favorite principle with him. Guilt wherever found ought to be punished. The Executive will have great opportunitys of abusing his power; particularly in time of war when the military force, and in some respects the public money will be in his hands. Should no regular punishment be provided, it will be irregularly inflicted by tumults and insurrections. He is aware of the necessity of proceeding with a cautious hand, and of excluding as much as possible the influence of the Legislature from the business. He suggested for consideration an idea which had fallen [from Col. Hamilton] of composing a forum out of the Judges belonging to the States; and even of requiring some preliminary inquest whether just grounds of impeachment existed. . . .

Mr. WILSON observed that if the idea were to be pursued, the Senators who are to hold their places during the same term with the Executive, ought to be subject to impeachment and removal.

Mr. PINKNEY apprehended that some gentlemen reasoned on a supposition that the Executive was to have powers which would not be committed to him. He presumed that his powers would be so circumscribed as to render impeachments unnecessary.

Mr. Govr. MORRIS'S opinion had been changed by the arguments used in the discussion. He was now sensible of the necessity of impeachments, if the Executive was to continue for any time in office. Our Executive was not like a Magistrate having a life interest, much less like one having an hereditary interest in his office. He may be bribed by a greater interest to betray his trust; and no one would say that we ought to expose ourselves to the danger of seeing the first Magistrate in foreign pay, without being able to guard against it by displacing him. One would think the King of England well secured against bribery. He has as it were a fee simple in the whole Kingdom. Yet Charles II was bribed by Louis XIV. The Executive ought therefore to be impeachable for treachery; corrupting his electors, and incapacity were other causes of impeachment. For the latter he should be punished not as a man, but as an officer, and punished only by degradation from his office. This Magistrate is not the King but the prime-Minister. The people are the King. When we make him amenable to Justice however we should take care to provide some mode that will not make him dependent on the Legislature.

It was moved and seconded to postpone the question of impeachments which was negatived. Mass. and S. Carolina only being ay.

On the Question, Shall the Executive be removeable on impeachments?

Mass. no. Conn. ay. N.J. ay. Pa. ay. Del. ay. Md. ay. Va. ay. N.C. ay. S.C. no. Geo. ay.

These and other questions were referred to a five-man Committee on Detail to iron out compromises and put together the finished Constitution. This committee included three future justices of the United States Supreme Court, Oliver Ellsworth of Connecticut, who was to be Chief Justice from 1796 to 1800, John Rutledge of South Carolina, and James Wilson of Pennsylvania. Their revision called for a single national executive, chosen for one seven-year term, ineligible a second time, and removable on impeachment by the House of Representatives and conviction by the supreme court for "treason, bribery, or corruption." The latter wording had replaced "mal-practice or neglect of duty."

In the floor debates on these revisions, the impeachment issue remained unresolved. Along with other matters, it was turned over to a special Committee of Eleven, which proposed more changes. Impeached officials would be tried in the Senate, with a two-thirds majority required for conviction. If the President was the defendant (the discussions all along assumed that judges should be impeachable), the Chief Justice would preside. Most important, the grounds for impeachment were changed again: corruption was dropped, leaving only treason and bribery.

MONDAY, AUGUST 27, 1787. IN CONVENTION

The clause for removing the President on impeachment by the House of Reps. and conviction in the supreme Court, of Treason, Bribery or corruption, was postponed at the instance of Mr. Govr. MORRIS, who thought the Tribunal an improper one, particularly, if the first judge was to be of the privy Council.

Mr. Govr. MORRIS objected also to the President of the Senate being provisional successor to the President, and suggested a designation of the Chief Justice.

Mr. MADISON added as a ground of objection that the Senate might retard the appointment of a President in order to carry points whilst the revisionary power was in the President of their own body, but suggested that the Executive powers during a vacancy, be administered by the persons composing the Council to the President.

Mr. WILLIAMSON suggested that the Legislature ought to have power to provide for occasional successors and moved that the last clause [of 2 sect. X art:] relating to a provisional successor to the President be postponed.

Mr. DICKINSON seconded the postponement, remarking that it was too vague. What is the extent of the term "disability" and who is to be the judge of it?

The postponement was agreed to . . .

Mr. DICKINSON moved as an amendment to sect. 2. art XI after the words "good behavior" the words "provided that they may be removed by the Executive on the application by the Senate and House of Representatives."

Mr. GERRY seconded the motion.

Mr. Govr. MORRIS thought it a contradiction in terms to say that the Judges should hold their offices during good behavior, and yet be removeable without a trial. Besides it was fundamentally wrong to subject Judges to so arbitrary an authority.

Mr. SHERMAN saw no contradiction or impropriety if this were made part of the constitutional regulation of the Judiciary establishment. He observed that a like provision was contained in the British Statutes. . . .

Mr. RANDOLPH opposed the motion as weakening too much the independence of the Judges.

Mr. DICKINSON was not apprehensive that the Legislature composed of different branches constructed on such different principles, would improperly unite for the purpose of displacing a Judge.

On the question for agreeing to Mr. Dickinson's Motion
N.H. no. Mass. abstain. Conn. ay. N.J. abstain. Pa. no. Del. no. Md. no. Va. no. N.C. abstain. S.C. no. Geo. no.

On the question of Sect. 2. art: XI as reported. Del. and Maryland only no. . . .

Sect. 3. art: XI being taken up, the following clause was postponed — viz. "to the trial of impeachments of officers of the U.S." by which the jurisdiction of the supreme Court was extended to such cases. . . .

The clause "in cases of impeachment," was postponed. . . .

FRIDAY, AUGUST 31, 1787

On motion of Mr. SHERMAN it was agreed to refer such parts of the Constitution as have been postponed, and such parts of Reports as have not been acted on, to a Committee of a member from each State; . . .

TUESDAY, SEPTEMBER 4, 1787. IN CONVENTION

Mr. BREARLY from the Committee of eleven made a further partial Report as follows:

The Committee of Eleven to whom sundry resolutions were referred on the 31st of August, report that in their opinion the following additions and alterations should be made to the Report before the Convention, viz. . . .

(3) In the place of the 9th art. Sect. I. to be inserted "The Senate of the U.S. shall have power to try all impeachments; but no person shall be convicted without the concurrence of two thirds of the members present. . . ."

(6) Sect. 3. The vice-president shall be ex officio President of the Senate, except when they sit to try the impeachment of the President, in which case the Chief Justice shall preside. . . .

The latter part of Sect. 2. Art: 10. to read as follows.

(9) He shall be removed from his office on impeachment by the House of Representatives, and conviction by the Senate, for Treason, or bribery, and in case of his removal as aforesaid, death, absence, resignation or inability to discharge the powers or duties of his office, the vice-president shall exercise those powers and duties until another President be chosen, or until the inability of the President be removed. . . .

The (3) clause was postponed in order to decide previously on the mode of electing the President.

These matters were debated again on September 8, and George Mason, one of the "lords of the Potomac" who was so active at the Convention, played a key role. Mason objected to restricting impeachment to only bribery and treason, because this would not include enough possible misdeeds; he wanted to limit the chief executive more. Mason fought hard at Philadephia to safeguard civil liberties against governmental abuses. Indeed, he refused to sign the completed Constitution, and later joined forces with Patrick Henry to oppose its ratification in Virginia because the new central government was not limited enough. Ironically, one of the few delegates who refused to sign the final document had much to do with the wording of the important impeachment provision. Mason proposed adding "maladministration" to bribery and treason, to broaden the range of impeachable offenses and thereby narrow the scope of presidential prerogatives. The scholarly Madison objected; the term was too vague. Mason thereupon withdrew that word, and proposed in its place "other high crimes and misdemeanors against the State." It was quickly approved. A brief discussion followed as some argued futilely that the Supreme Court rather than the Senate should try impeached officials. Then two more changes were made. "United States" replaced "State" to remove any ambiguity, and almost as an afterthought the words "vice-President and other Civil officers of the United States" were added to the list of impeachable officials.

SATURDAY, SEPTEMBER 8. IN CONVENTION

The last Report of Committee of Eleven was resumed.

The clause referring to the Senate, the trial of impeachments against the President, for Treason and bribery, was taken up.

Col. MASON. Why is the provision restrained to Treason and bribery only? Treason as defined in the Constitution will not reach many great and dangerous offences. Hastings is not guilty of Treason. Attempts to subvert the Constitution may not be Treason as above defined. As bills of attainder which have saved the British Constitution are forbidden, it is the more necessary to extend: the power of impeachments. He moved to add after "bribery" "or maladministration." Mr. GERRY seconded him.

Mr. MADISON. So vague a term will be equivalent to a tenure during pleasure of the Senate.

Mr. Govr. MORRIS. It will not be put in force and can do no harm. An election of every four years will prevent maladministration.

Col. MASON withdrew "maladministration" and substitutes "other high crimes and misdemeanors against the State."

On the question thus altered

N.H. ay. Mass. ay. Conn. ay. N.J. no. Pa. no. Del. no. Md. ay. Va. ay. N.C. ay. S.C. ay. Geo. ay.

Mr. MADISON, objected to a trial of the President by the Senate, especially as he was to be impeached by the other branch of the Legislature, and for any act which might be called a misdemeanor. The President under these circumstances was made improperly dependent. He would prefer the Supreme Court for the trial of impeachments, or rather a tribunal of which that should form a part.

Mr. Govr. MORRIS thought no other tribunal than the Senate could be trusted. The supreme Court were too few in number and might be warped or corrupted. He was against a dependence of the Executive on the Legislature, considering the Legislative tyranny the great danger to be apprehended; but there could be no danger that the Senate would say untruly on their oaths that the President was guilty of crimes or facts, especially as in four years he can be turned out.

Mr. PINKNEY disapproved of making the Senate the Court of Impeachments, as rendering the President too dependent on the Legislature. If he opposes a favorite law, the two Houses will combine against him, and under the influence of heat and faction throw him out of office.

Mr. WILLIAMSON thought there was more danger of too much lenity than too much rigour towards the President, considering the number of cases in which the Senate was associated with the President.

Mr. SHERMAN regarded the Supreme Court as improper to try the President, because the Judges would be appointed by him.

On motion by Mr. MADISON to strike out the words — "by the Senate" after the word "conviction."

N.H. no. Mass. no. Conn. no. N.J. no. Pa. ay. Del. no. Md. no. Va. ay. N.C. no. S.C. no. Geo. no.

In the amendment of Col. Mason just agreed to, the word "State" after the words "misdemeanors against" was struck out, and the words "United States" inserted unanimously, in order to remove ambiguity.

On the question to agree to clause as amended,

N.H. ay. Mass. ay. Conn. ay. N.J. ay. Pa. no. Del. ay. Md. ay. Va. ay. N.C. ay. S.C. ay. Geo. ay.

On motion "The vice-President and other Civil officers of the U.S. shall be removed from office on impeachment and conviction as aforesaid" was added to the clause on the subject of impeachment. . . .

It is intriguing that without any serious objection "other high crimes and misdemeanors" was readily substituted for "maladministration" because "maladministration" was too vague. Apparently, however, the phrase "high crimes and misdemeanors" was clear. To understand why, we must turn again to English history and English law.

Students of England's legal and judicial history have verified that in 1787 "high crimes and misdemeanors" was a category of *political* crimes against the state. Because "crimes and misdemeanors" is a familiar term of criminal law, it is easy to conclude that "high" crimes and misdemeanors are simply "more serious" crimes and misdemeanors. That is not so. The word "high" meant something altogether different in the English judicial lexicon. It was a technical legal term. Without it, "crimes and misdemeanors" represented a category of relatively minor criminal offenses. With it, "high crimes and [high] misdemeanors" was a very serious charge that bordered on treason. An examination of English impeachment cases, especially those of the Stuart period with which the framers were so familiar, reveals that many were based on non-criminal misconduct, and that "high crimes and misdemeanors" were essentially political offenses rather than criminal. Among such impeachable offenses were: applying funds to purposes other than those specified, procuring offices for persons unfit and unworthy of them, delaying justice by interfering with certain writs, procuring titles and other benefits for relatives, reviling and threatening a grand jury, interfering with election procedures, arbitrarily granting blank general warrants, and even using one's office and influence to obtain property for less than its actual value. The noted scholar Raoul Berger divides "high crimes and misdemeanors" into four clearly identifiable categories: (1) misapplication of funds, (2) abuse of official power, (3) neglect of duty, and (4) encroachment on or contempts of Parliament's prerogatives. A fifth more general category, corruption, included such offenses as betrayal of trust, obtaining property for less than its value through official influence, procuring large gifts, and giving pernicious advice. When the Framers used the term "high crimes and misdemeanors," they were referring to specific categories of offenses, and they deliberately used terminology with a known technical and limited meaning.

The dilemma which the Framers faced was that they wanted the chief executive to be both independent *and* responsible. They wanted to be able to remove him, but the English system — responsibility to Parliament through a vote of confidence — was out of the question if they were to preserve separation of powers and an independent President. By adapting the impeachment procedure to the new American system, they could achieve these ends. Thus they established a President who was independent but who still could be removed by Congress if he became a tyrant. But to protect against *legislative* tyranny in the abuse of this removal power, they avoided vague terminology such as "maladministration" or "corruption," and carefully worded the grounds for impeachment to include only offenses which were clearly identifiable in the law as they understood it: treason, bribery, and high crimes and misdemeanors.

Drafting the Constitution was only one step toward establishing the new government; next came the struggle for ratification. Conventions met (in all states except Rhode Island, which had boycotted the Philadelphia meeting), and the deliberations were intense and heated. They dealt with issues ranging from the broad nature and philosophy of the proposed federal system to seemingly picayune and inconsequential details. Many questions were raised, many criticisms were voiced, many defenses were promulgated. Not the least of the discussions centered on the impeachment provision. Some felt it might interfere with executive independence; others argued for removal by the courts; some wanted only clarification. The discussions at the ratifying convention in North Carolina are typical. Among the participants, Richard Dobbs Spaight had attended the Constitutional Convention as a delegate and had signed the completed Constitution, while James Iredell had not been a delegate, but was to be among the first appointed to the new United States Supreme Court. His observation that impeachment "must be for an error of the heart, and not of the head" is most cogent. The views expressed in this discussion reflect many similar questions raised later about what actions justify impeachment. (These excerpts are from Jonathan Elliot (ed.), *The Debates in the Several State Conventions on the Adoption of the Federal Convention*, IV).

Mr. JOSEPH TAYLOR objected to the provision made for impeaching. He urged that there could be no security from it, as the persons accused were triable by the Senate, who were a part of the legislature themselves; that, while men were fallible, the senators were liable to errors, especially in a case where they were concerned themselves.

Mr. IREDELL. Mr. Chairman, I was going to observe that this clause, vesting the power of impeachment in the House of Representatives, is one of the greatest securities for a due execution of all public offices. Every government requires it. Every man ought to be amenable for his conduct, and there are no persons so proper to complain of the public officers as the representatives of the people at large. ... If this power were not provided, the consequences might be fatal. It will be not only the means of punishing misconduct, but it will prevent misconduct. A man in public office who knows that there is no tribunal to punish him, may be ready to deviate from his duty; but if he knows there is a tribunal for that purpose, although he may be a man of no principle, the very terror of punishment will perhaps deter him. . . .

Mr. BLOODWORTH wished to be informed, whether this sole power of impeachment, given to the House of Representatives, deprived the state of the power of impeaching any of its members.

Mr. SPAIGHT answered, that this impeachment extended only to the officers of the United States — that it would be improper if the same body that impeached had the power of trying — that, therefore, the Constitution had wisely given the power of impeachment to the House of Representatives, and that of trying impeachments to the Senate.

Mr. JOSEPH TAYLOR. Mr. Chairman, the objection is very strong. If there be but one body to try, where are we? If any tyranny or oppression should arise, how are those who perpetrated such oppression to be tried and punished? By a tribunal consisting of the very men who assist in such tyranny. Can any tribunal be found, in any community, who will give judgment against their own actions? Is it the nature of man to decide against himself? . . . None can impeach but the representatives; and the impeachments are to be determined by the senators, who are one of the branches of power which we dread under this Constitution.

His excellency, Govr. JOHNSTON. Mr. Chairman, . . . I never knew any instance of a man being impeached for a legislative act; nay, I never heard it suggested before. No member of the House of Commons, in England, has ever been impeached before the Lords, nor any lord, for a legislative misdemeanor. A representative is answerable to no power but his constituents. He is accountable to no being under heaven but the people who appointed him. . . .

Mr. BLOODWORTH observed, that as this was a Constitution for the United States, he should not have made the observation he did, had the subject not been particularly mentioned — that the words "sole power of impeachment" were so general, and might admit of such a latitude of construction, as to extend to every legislative member upon the continent, so as to preclude the representatives of the different states from impeaching.

Mr. MACLAINE. Mr. Chairman, if I understand the gentleman rightly, he means that Congress may impeach all the people or officers of the United States. If the gentleman will attend, he will see that this is a government for confederated states; that, consequently, it can never inter-meddle

where no power is given. I confess I can see no more reason
to fear in this case than from our own General Assembly. A
power is given to our own state Senate to try impeachments. . . . Should there not be some mode of punishment
for the offences of the officers of the general government?
Is it not necessary that such officers should be kept within
proper bounds? . . .

Mr. IREDELL. Mr. Chairman, the objections to this
clause deserve great consideration. . . . It is objected to as
improper, because, if the President or Senate should abuse
their trust, there is not sufficient responsibility, since he
can only be tried by the Senate, by whose advice he acted;
and the Senate cannot be tried at all. I beg leave to observe
that, when any man is impeached, it must be for an error of
the heart, and not of the head. God forbid that a man, in
any country in the world, should be liable to be punished
for want of judgment. This is not the case here. As to errors
of the heart, there is sufficient responsibility. Should these
be committed, there is a ready way to bring him to punishment. This is a responsibility which answers every purpose
that could be desired by a people jealous of their liberty. I
presume that, if the President, with the advice of the
Senate, should make a treaty with a foreign power, and that
treaty should be deemed unwise, or against the interest of
the country, yet if nothing could be objected against it but
the difference of opinion between them and their constituents, they could not justly be obnoxious to punishment. If
they were punishable for exercising their own judgment,
and not that of their constituents, no man who regarded his
reputation would accept the office either of a senator or
President. Whatever mistake a man may make, he ought not
to be punished for it, nor his posterity rendered infamous.
But if a man be a villain, and wilfully abuse his trust, he is
to be held up as a public offender, and ignominiously
punished. A public officer ought not to act from a principle
of fear. Were he punishable for want of judgment, he would
be continually in dread; but when he knows that nothing
but real guilt can disgrace him, he may do his duty firmly,
if he be an honest man; and if he be not, a just fear of
disgrace may, perhaps, as to the public, have nearly the
effect of an intrinsic principle of virtue. According to these
principles, I suppose the only instances, in which the President would be liable to impeachment, would be where he
had received a bribe, or had acted from some corrupt
motive or other. . . . The President must certainly be punishable for giving false information to the Senate. He is to
regulate all intercourse with foreign powers, and it is his
duty to impart to the Senate every material intelligence he

receives. If it should appear that he has not given them full information, but has concealed important intelligence which he ought to have communicated, and by that means induced them to enter into measures injurious to their country, and which they would not have consented to had the true state of things been disclosed to them, — in this case, I ask whether, upon an impeachment for a misdemeanor upon such an account, the Senate would probably favor him. . . .

The struggle for ratification was carried on also by letter-writers, editorialists and pamphleteers. One was Richard Henry Lee of Virginia. Lee had refused to be a delegate to Philadelphia because he anticipated a strong central government would be formulated there. He favored state sovereignty as it existed under the Articles of Confederation, and became a foremost opponent to ratification of the Constitution. In a series of articles entitled *Letters of a Federal Farmer*, he included, among other criticisms, an attack on the impeachment provision as unworkable. Except for elected officials, he observed, all "civil officers of the United States" would be appointed by the President and approved by the Senate. If any of them were impeached, they would be tried by the same body, the Senate, which had approved them earlier. Certainly two-thirds of the Senators would never admit to such a judgmental error, Lee argued, and for that reason the House probably never or seldom would exercise its impeachment power in the first place.

The most important literature of the ratification period, of course, was the *Federalist Papers*. Written by Alexander Hamilton, John Jay, and James Madison, these eighty-five essays (a majority by Hamilton) were written primarily to urge ratification in New York. The literary style of the essays was in the form of refutation of arguments of opponents to the Constitution; the result was a classic of American political thought. It was the first important interpretation of the Constitution and the first significant analysis of modern federalism.

Included in this interpretation and analysis were meaningful observations about impeachment. Hamilton expressed serious concern about factionalism, and recognized that a presidential impeachment proceeding could have a divisive effect upon the country. But when he weighed the dangers of a splintered community against a despotic executive, he concluded that the latter was more dangerous. Significantly, Hamilton had no doubts about what actions warranted impeachment: "The subjects of its jurisdiction," he wrote in *The Federalist* No. 65, "are those offenses which proceed from the misconduct of public men, or in other words from the abuse or violation of some public trust. They are of a nature which may with peculiar propriety be denominated POLITICAL, as they relate chiefly to injuries done immediately to the society itself." An indictable criminal act would of course subject the chief executive to removal proceedings; but Hamilton argued for safeguards against political improprieties as well. Even if impeachment "agitate[d] the passions" and divided the country, it was still preferable to leaving a tyrant in office.

THE FEDERALIST NO. 65

A well constituted court for the trial of impeachments, is an object not more to be desired than difficult to be obtained in a government wholly elective. The subjects of its jurisdiction are those offenses which proceed from the misconduct of public men, or in other words from the abuse or violation of some public trust. They are of a nature which may with peculiar propriety be denominated POLITICAL, as they relate chiefly to injuries done immediately to the society itself. The prosecution of them, for this reason, will seldom fail to agitate the passions of the whole community, and to divide it into parties, more or less friendly or inimical, to the accused. In many cases, it will connect itself with the pre-existing factions, and will enlist all their animosities, partialities, influence and interest on one side, or on the other; and in such cases there will always be the greatest danger, that the decision will be regulated more by the comparative strength of parties than by the real demonstrations of innocence or guilt.

The delicacy and magnitude of a trust, which so deeply concerns the political reputation and existence of every man engaged in the administration of public affairs, speak for themselves. The difficulty of placing it rightly in a government resting entirely on the basis of periodical elections will as readily be perceived, when it is considered that the most conspicuous characters in it will, from that circumstance, be too often the leaders, or the tools of the most cunning or the most numerous faction; and on this account can hardly be expected to possess the requisite neutrality towards those, whose conduct may be the subject of scrutiny. . . .

What it may be asked is the true spirit of the institution itself? Is it not designed as a method of NATIONAL IN-QUEST into the conduct of public men? If this be the design of it, who can so properly be the inquisitors for the nation, as the representatives of the nation themselves? It is not disputed that the power of originating the inquiry, or in other words of preferring the impeachment ought to be lodged in the hands of one branch of the legislative body; will not the reasons which indicate the propriety of this arrangement, strongly plead for an admission of the other branch of that body to a share in the inquiry? The model, from which the idea of this institution has been borrowed, pointed out that course to the Convention: In Great Britain, it is the province of the house of commons to prefer the impeachments; and of the house of lords to decide upon it. Several of the State constitutions have followed the example. As well the latter as the former seem to have regarded the practice of impeachments, as a bridle in the hands of the legislative body upon the executive servants of the government. Is not this the true light in which it ought to be regarded?

Where else, than in the Senate could have been found a tribunal sufficiently dignified, or sufficiently independent? What other body would be likely to feel *confidence enough in its own situation*, to preserve unawed and uninfluenced the necessary impartiality between an *individual* accused, and the *representatives of the people, his accusers?*

Could the Supreme Court have been relied upon as answering this description? It is much to be doubted whether the members of that tribunal would, at all times, be endowed with so eminent a portion of fortitude, as would be called for in the execution of so difficult a task; and it is still more to be doubted, whether they would possess the degree of credit and authority, which might, on certain occasions, be indispensable, towards reconciling the people to a decision, that should happen to clash with an accusation brought by their immediate representatives. A deficiency in the first would be fatal to the accused; in the last, dangerous to the public tranquillity. . . . The necessity of a numerous court for the trial of impeachments is equally dictated by the nature of the proceeding. This can never be tied down by such strict rules, either in the delineation of the offence by the prosecutors, or in the construction of it by the Judges, as in common cases serve to limit the discretion of courts in favor of personal security. There will be no jury to stand between the Judges, who are to pronounce the sentence of the law and the party who is to receive or suffer it. The awful discretion, which a court of impeachments must necessarily have, to doom to honor or to infamy the most confidential and the most distinguished characters of the community, forbids the commitment of the trust to a small number of persons.

These considerations seem alone sufficient to authorise a conclusion, that the Supreme Court would have been an improper substitute for the Senate, as a court of impeachments. There remains a further consideration which will not a little strengthen this conclusion. It is this. The punishment, which may be the consequence of conviction upon impeachment, is not to terminate the chastisement of the offender. After having been sentenced to a perpetual ostracism from the esteem and confidence, and honors and emoluments of his country, he will still be liable to prosecution and punishment in the ordinary course of law. Would it be proper that the persons, who had disposed of his fame and his most valuable rights as a citizen in one trial, should in another trial, for the same offence, be also the disposers of his life and his fortune? . . .

Would it have been an improvement of the plan, to have united the Supreme Court with the Senate, in the formation of the court of impeachments? This Union would certainly have been attended with several advantages; but would they not have been overbalanced by the signal disadvantage, already stated, arising from the agency of the same Judges in the double prosecution to which the offender would be liable? To a certain extent, the benefits of that Union will be obtained from making the Chief Justice of the Supreme Court the President of the court of impeachments, as is proposed to be done in the plan of the Convention; while the inconveniences of an entire incorporation of the former into the latter will be substantially avoided. This was perhaps the prudent mean. . . .

Would it have been desirable to have composed the court for the trial of impeachments of persons wholly distinct from the other departments of the government? . . . To some minds, it will not appear a trivial objection, that it would tend to increase the complexity of the political machine; and to add a new spring to the government, the utility of which would at best be questionable. But an objection, which will not be thought by any unworthy of attention, is this — A court formed upon such a plan would either be attended with heavy expence, or might in practice be subject to a variety of casualties and inconveniencies. It must either consist of permanent officers stationary at the seat of government, and of course entitled to fixed and regular stipends, or of certain officers of the State governments, to be called upon whenever an impeachment was actually depending. It will not be easy to imagine any third mode materially different, which could rationally be proposed. . . .

In response to arguments that the Supreme Court, not the Senate, should try the accused official, Hamilton carefully analyzed the dual legislative and judicial character of the Senate, and in *The Federalist* Nos. 51, 65, and 66 systematically struck down these criticisms. Complemented with arguments in Nos. 78 and 80 defending the "good behavior" tenure of judges, this remains the classic statement of the role of the Senate and the federal judiciary in the impeachment process and in their balance of power relationship.

THE FEDERALIST NO. 66

A review of the principal objections that have appeared against the proposed court for the trial of impeachments, . . .

The *first* of these objections is, that the provision in question confounds legislative and judiciary authorities in the same body; in violation of that important and well established maxim, which requires a separation between the different departments of power. The true meaning of this maxim has been discussed and ascertained in another place, [Nos. 47-52], and has been shown to be entirely compatible with a partial intermixture of those departments for special purposes, preserving them in the main distinct and unconnected. This partial intermixture is even in some cases not only proper, but necessary to the mutual defence of the several members of the government, against each other. An absolute or qualified negative in the executive, upon the acts of the legislative body, is admitted by the ablest adepts in political science, to be an indefensible barrier against the encroachments of the latter upon the former. And it may perhaps with not less reason be contended that the powers relating to impeachments are as before intimated, an essential check in the hands of that body upon the encroachments of the executive. The division of them between the two branches of the legislature; assigning to one the right of accusing, to the other the right of judging; avoids the inconvenience of making the same persons both accusers and judges; and guards against the danger of persecution from the prevalency of a factious spirit in either of those branches. As the concurrence of two-thirds of the senate will be requisite to a condemnation, the security to innocence, from this additional circumstance, will be as complete as itself can desire. . . .

A *second* objection to the senate, as a court of impeachments, is, that it contributes to an undue accumulation of power in that body, tending to give to the government a countenance too aristocratic. The senate, it is observed, is to have concurrent authority with the executive in the formation of treaties, and in the appointment to offices: If, say the objectors, to these prerogatives is added that of deciding in all cases of impeachment, it will give a decided predominancy to senatorial influence. To an objection so little precise in itself, it is not easy to find a very precise answer. . . . [There then follow arguments that various powers of the executive and of the House of Representatives balance powers of the Senate.]

A third objection to the senate as a court of impeachments is drawn from the agency they are to have in the appointments to office. It is imagined that they would be too indulgent judges of the conduct of men, in whose official creation they had participated. The principle of this objection would condemn a practice, which is to be seen in all the state governments, if not in all the governments, with which we are acquainted: I mean that of rendering those, who hold office during pleasure, dependent on the pleasure of those, who appoint them. With equal plausibility might it be alledged in this case that the favoritism of the latter would always be an asylum for the misbehavior of the former. But that practice, in contradiction to this principle, proceeds upon the presumption, that the responsibility of those who appoint, for the fitness and competency of the persons, on whom they bestow their choice, and the interest they will have in the respectable and prosperous administration of affairs, will inspire a sufficient disposition, to dismiss from a share in it, all such, who, by their conduct, shall have proved themselves unworthy of the confidence reposed in them. Though facts may not always correspond with this presumption, yet if it be in the main just, it must destroy the supposition, that the senate, who will merely sanction the choice of the executive, should feel a bias towards the objects of that choice, strong enough to blind them to the evidences of guilt so extraordinary as to have induced the representatives of the nation to become its accusers. . . .

A fourth objection to the senate, in the capacity of a court of impeachments, is derived from their union with the executive in the power of making treaties. This, it has been said, would constitute the senators their own judges, in every case of a corrupt or perfidious execution of that trust. After having combined with the executive in betraying the interests of the nation in a ruinous treaty, what prospect, it is asked, would there be of their being made to suffer the punishment, they would deserve, when they were themselves to decide upon the accusation brought against them for the treachery of which they had been guilty?

This objection has been circulated with more earnestness and with greater show of reason, than any other which has appeared against this part of the plan; and yet I am deceived if it does not rest upon an erroneous foundation. . . . The security to the society must depend on the care which is taken to confide the trust to proper hands, to make it their interest to execute it with fidelity, and to make it as difficult as possible for them to combine in any interest opposite to that of the public good. . . .

The adoption of the Constitution was assured in the summer of 1788 when New Hampshire became the ninth state to ratify, followed shortly by Virginia and New York. Immediately steps were taken to initiate the new government as Representatives, Senators, and presidential electors were chosen. In April, 1789, the Washington administration and the first Congress organized for business. The Constitution was in operation. Waiting in the wings, if needed, were its watchdog impeachment provisions:

Article I; Section 2, clause 5
The House of Representatives . . . shall have the sole Power of Impeachment.

Article I; Section 3, clauses 6 and 7
The Senate shall have the sole Power to try all Impeachments. When sitting for that Purpose, they shall be in Oath or Affirmation. When the President of the United States is tried, the Chief Justice shall preside; and no person shall be convicted without the concurrence of two thirds of the Members present.

Judgment in Cases of Impeachment shall not extend further than to removal from Office, and disqualification to hold and enjoy any Office of honor, Trust or Profit under the United States; but the Party convicted shall nevertheless be liable and subject to Indictment, Trial, Judgment and Punishment, according to Law.

Article II; Section 2, clause 1
The President . . . shall have Power to grant Reprieves and Pardons for Offenses against the United States, except in cases of Impeachment.

Article II; Section 4

The President, Vice-President and all civil Officers of the United States, shall be removed from Office on Impeachment for, and Conviction of, Treason, Bribery, or other high Crimes and Misdemeanors.

Article III; Section 2, clause 3

The Trial of all Crimes, except in Cases of Impeachment, shall be by Jury.

2
Impeachments and Trials

The history of impeachment in the United States since 1789 probably would astound the Founding Fathers. One of their major concerns was that a President might become a despot. Sufficient precedent existed to cope with judicial tyranny; the Framers agreed overwhelmingly that miscreant judges should be impeached and, sadly, that some undoubtedly would be. But their greatest fear was of executive tyranny. Yet only once has impeachment involved a President; the others were civil officers, mostly judges.

Impeachment proceedings have been initiated in the House of Representatives more than fifty times, but only twelve cases have reached the Senate. One involved President Andrew Johnson; one involved a United States Senator; one, a member of the cabinet; the remaining nine were federal judges, including one Associate Justice of the Supreme Court. Six cases ended in acquittal, two were dismissed for lack of jurisdiction, and four ended in conviction. All four were lower federal judges.[1]

The first impeachment attempt proved abortive. In April, 1796, residents of the Northwest Territory petitioned the House of Representatives, accusing territorial Judge George Turner of arbitrary misconduct. The petition was referred briefly to a special House committee, then to Attorney General Charles Lee. When Lee indicated that the territorial courts would prosecute, proceedings in the House were terminated.

The Turner case provided neither criteria nor precedents. At various times impeachments have been initiated by resolution introduced by a Representative, by letter or message from the President, or by grand jury action. The five cases to reach the Senate since 1900, for instance, emanated from resolutions initiated by the House Judiciary Committee. Many practices were adapted from British precedents; others developed as impeachments occurred. Especially unusual is the title "Managers" for those Representatives who prosecute the case when it goes to trial in the Senate. The term comes from *Jefferson's Manual of Parliamentary Practice*, one of the sources of parliamentary rules in the House of Representatives. (See the Appendix for this and other procedures followed in the House and Senate during impeachment and trial.)

The next impeachment attempt was against Senator William Blount of Tennessee. A native of North Carolina, Blount had an imposing background. He had been a veteran of the Revolutionary War, a member of the Continental Congress, a delegate from North Carolina to the Constitutional Convention and signer of the Constitution, Governor of the Territory South of the River Ohio, and Superintendent of Indian Affairs. He was chairman of the convention which framed the first state constitution for Tennessee, and that state's first Senator when it was admitted to the Union. But on July 3, 1797, President John Adams sent to both the House and the Senate letters accusing Blount of conspiring to help England gain control of Spanish territory in Florida and Louisiana. For the first time in its history the House voted impeachment charges, necessitating a trial in the Senate. A summary of the salient facts of the Blount case, as well as of the other impeachment cases, will be found at the end of this chapter.

The Blount impeachment and trial raised several significant questions. As a Senator, was Blount a "civil officer" subject to impeachment under the Constitution? The day after the House approved impeachment, but before Articles were drawn up, the Senate, acting independently on President Adams' accusations, expelled Blount. Did this affect the trial in the Senate? If Blount was still subject to impeachment, was it as a Senator or as a private citizen? Indeed, could a private citizen even be impeached and tried?

Blount adopted the jurisdictional defense that Senators could not be impeached, arguing that the word "civil" in the phrase "all civil Officers" in the Constitution merely exempted military officers from the double indignity of impeachment after a court martial. Blount's counsel, the eminent Philadelphia lawyers Alexander J. Dallas and Jared Ingersoll, argued that if the Framers of the Constitution had intended to include Senators and Representatives, they would have done so explicitly. Instead, they had provided elsewhere for removal of Congressmen, authorizing each house to expel its own members. These arguments conflict with statements at the Constitutional Convention, at state ratifying meetings, and in *The Federalist* No. 66, which suggest that Senators were impeachable. Indeed, House Managers who prosecuted, led by James A. Bayard and Robert Goodloe Harper, argued that *"all* civil Officers" meant precisely what it said.

On January 11, 1799, the Senate dismissed all charges against Blount on the grounds that a Senator was not a civil officer within the meaning of the impeachment clause of the Constitution. Had they decided the case on its merits, undoubtedly Blount would have been found guilty; but the decision was based on jurisdiction. In a recent study, historian Irving Brant concludes that the Senate's decision reflected political rather than legal considerations.[2] He suggests that the Blount impeachment was a part of the Federalist Party's anti-foreign and anti-liberal campaign. During the 1790's the repercussions of the French Revolution were keenly felt in the United States. The revolt against royal despotism begun in 1789 had turned into a European social war and blood bath. Especially after hostilities began in 1793 between France and England, American opinion was polarized between Jeffersonian Republicans who defended the French Revolution in spite of its excesses and Federalists who feared a similar bloody denouement in the United States. Fearful lest "Jacobin terror" invade this country, conservative Federalists pushed through measures to "safeguard home and hearth." Among these were an Alien Act to expel "dangerous" foreigners, and a Sedition Act to silence "libellous" journalists. The capstone was a Senate resolution, introduced by Jacob Read of South Carolina, which would have subjected certain private citizens, in addition to the "President, Vice-President, and all civil Officers," to the impeachment provisions of the Constitution. Conviction of Blount as a private citizen would set a precedent, making "dangerous" Americans "liable to perpetual exclusion from office by expansive interpretation of the constitutional clause on impeachment." Both the Senate resolution and the drive to convict Blount failed, however, because not enough Federalists would go so far. Instead, they took a simpler way out. Blount already had been punished (expelled) for his intrigue and chicanery; a jurisdictional dismissal would evade the political cauldron. By a vote of 14-11, therefore, all charges against Blount were dismissed on the grounds that the impeachment clause did not apply to members of Congress. The Senators thus avoided a political brawl, but in the process they subverted the principle of the Framers that *all* civil officers of the United States were subject to impeachment and conviction. That precedent, that members of Congress are not subject to impeachment, still prevails.

If partisanship was avoided in the Blount case, it emerged full-blown in the next two impeachments involving Judges John Pickering and Samuel Chase. As a result of the election of 1800 the Republicans threw the Federalists out of office, except for the judiciary. According to the Constitution, federal judges are appointed by the President for life, and can be removed forcibly only for a violation of "good behavior." Prior to Jefferson's election, all these appointments had been made by Federalist Presidents Washington and John Adams. Republicans had become stirred up over what they saw as Federalist judicial partisanship. When Republican journalists were jailed for sedition, Jeffersonians cried "Tyranny!" while Federalists replied "Treason!" Three prominent Republican editors, Thomas Cooper, James Callender, and William Duane, were prosecuted for "Jacobinism" in trials noteworthy for grossly partisan conduct by Federalist judges, among them Supreme Court Justice Samuel Chase. Republican frustrations were compounded by the Judiciary Act passed by the lame-duck Federalist Congress in 1801 and by President Adams' appointment of Federalist "midnight judges" to strengthen the defeated party's grip on the judicial branch of the government. One outraged Kentucky Republican denounced this as "the last effort of the most wicked, insidious and turbulent faction that ever disgraced our political annals."

Jeffersonians were determined to make a change, and some saw impeachment as a solution. The misdeed in the Blount case was indisputable; but what "offenses" had

Federalist judges committed? Some angry Jeffersonians were willing to interpret "high crimes and misdemeanors" so broadly that judges could be removed even if out of step with public opinion. "Good behavior" would be defined by a majority of the House and two thirds of the Senate. After all, insisted William Giles, one of the Jeffersonian leaders in the Senate, "impeachment is nothing more than an inquiry by the two Houses of Congress, whether the office of any public man might not be better filled by another." Federalists argued that judges should be above politics; Republicans countered that by their actions many Federalist judges already had entered the political arena. Some Jeffersonians advocated moderation, but even they were willing to interpret "high crimes and misdemeanors" broadly enough to include questionable judicial ethics or misconduct on the bench. Certain judges had rendered grossly partisan decisions; some had participated imprudently in political campaigns or had issued intemperate political harangues from the bench. Justice Samuel Chase, for instance, had campaigned openly for President Adams before a jury. Moderate Republicans considered these properly impeachable offenses. That the offending judge was a Federalist may have been only coincidental. It probably was not. But what was incontrovertible was that those who considered impeachment a *political* instrument against governmental oppression could find considerable support in history and in the intent of the Founding Fathers. This indeed is how impeachment originated, how it developed, and why it was included in the Constitution. The dilemma was where to draw the fine distinction between impeachable political oppression by Federalist judges, and partisan political retribution by accusing Jeffersonians.

The first confrontation was the impeachment of District Judge John Pickering in 1803. Pickering was an ill-mannered and repulsive individual, perhaps because of a mental illness described by contemporaries as "insanity." He often disgraced his court by his profanity and intoxication. In the case which precipitated his impeachment charges, he was so incoherent during one session that the proceedings had to be postponed until the following morning so he could sober up. The next day he was worse. Perhaps Americans should be the last to complain about swearing and drinking — but not by a judge on the bench. Certainly in Pickering's case it resulted in questionable legal irregularities and indiscretions. By most standards, John Pickering was a poor judge. He was also an openly partisan Federalist.

The cornerstone of Pickering's defense was that he was insane and that the Constitution did not make "incapacity" grounds for impeachment. This was a possible jurisdictional escape as in the Blount case. But it was precisely because of this insanity that Pickering was convicted — not clinical insanity, which would have opened a Pandora's box, but rather his scandalous performance on the bench. Jeffersonians equated this with the Constitutional "good behavior" *proviso* for removal. Federalists cried foul partisanship, though many conceded that Pickering did deserve conviction. No one knows how many Senators cast their votes on the historic premise that impeachment was a justifiable political action to remove a judicial tyrant, how many voted as partisan Federalists and Republicans, or how many rationalized conviction as a merciful way to remove a sick man from the bench. But Pickering was convicted by a two-thirds vote and removed.

On March 12, 1804, at the same hour that Pickering was convicted in the Senate, Supreme Court Justice Samuel Chase was impeached in the House of Representatives. The circumstances leading to Chase's impeachment were similar to those in Pickering's case — injudicious participation in political activities, and gross partisanship and questionable personal conduct on the bench. Labelled a "ringleader of mobs, a foul mouthed and inflaming son of discord" when he led the Sons of Liberty, Chase in pre-Revolutionary days had given every indication of becoming an ardent egalitarian and champion of individual rights. Instead he became one of the foremost symbols of judicial tyranny. "A licentious press," he wrote in 1796, "is the bane of freedom" — when that press dared to criticize the government. Appointed to the Supreme Court by President Washington, Chase did not hide his partisanship. He campaigned openly for the Federalist John Adams, and reputedly "tried Republicans without mercy." He attacked the Jefferson administration and its doctrines publicly and contemptuously; in 1803, for instance, he told a Baltimore grand jury that the dangerous Jeffersonian policies of "equal liberties and equal rights" would "take away all security for property and personal liberty . . . and our republican constitution will sink into a mobocracy, the worst of all popular governments." The names, places, and specifics differed, but the generalities applicable to the impeachment of Pickering were the same for Chase, except that Chase had no mental incapacities. But Chase was acquitted.

On the basis of the Pickering outcome, Chase also should have been convicted. He was as obnoxious and repressive on the bench as Pickering. If Pickering's judicial tyranny merited conviction, the acquittal of Chase was a travesty on justice. Yet it long has been characterized as a triumph of justice over heated political partisanship, a key event in the elimination of impeachment as a devious political weapon to coerce legitimate opposition.

A reappraisal of Chase's acquittal indicates that it does not belong on such a high level of domestic statesmanship. If Chase's impeachment in the House was the result of Republican partisanship, then his acquittal in the Senate was no less Federalist partisanship. All Federalist Senators supported him consistently.[3] Another reason for Chase's acquittal was the surprisingly poor case made by the House Managers. Legalists are appalled at the shallow arguments by such otherwise brilliant lawyers as Caesar A. Rodney of Delaware (later Jefferson's Attorney General) and Joseph H. Nicholson of Maryland (later a federal judge). Further-more, the shrill-voiced and violent-tempered John Randolph of Virginia, chairman of the House Managers, badgered and confused the proceedings with nonessential and immaterial arguments. The House Managers simply made a weak case where many agree they had the weight of both the evidence and the law on their side.

The main reason, though, why the Chase acquittal merits reappraisal is the role it played in confounding the fundamental nature of impeachment. As indicated previously, impeachment as understood by the Framers of the Con-stitution was not a criminal litigation. It was a political procedure used to remove officials who committed either a *criminal* or a *non-criminal* wrong. The reason for the phrase "high crimes and misdemeanors" was to limit the non-criminal offenses to a known entity rather than to the vagueness of such terms as "mal-practice" or "maladministration." If the misdeed was criminal in nature, criminal litigation could be instituted in the regular courts *after* removal from office. There was nothing in precedent or law that limited impeachment only to criminal offenses. Yet in the Chase trial, that was precisely the defense presented by Joseph Hopkinson and Luther Martin — and the House Managers' weak response lent credibility to the argument. Chase was acquitted because enough Senators became convinced that his partisan misuse of judicial power was not an indictable crime. This narrow interpretation of "high crimes and misdemeanors" greatly weakened the impeachment safeguard placed in the Constitution because it created the misconception that an official was impeachable only if he had committed an indictable criminal act. This doctrine was not abandoned until the twentieth century. In the meantime, it saved one President, Andrew Johnson, from conviction and removal from office, and it contributed to so much misunderstanding and confusion about the Johnson case that many became skeptical of impeachment as a viable procedure for removing an erring President.

The impact of the Chase acquittal was evident in the next case to reach the Senate. In 1830 Judge James H. Peck of the Missouri District Court was impeached for alleged criminal misconduct in suspending and jailing a lawyer who had written a critical newspaper article. House Managers, including Pennsylvania Congressman James Buchanan, whose reputation as a lawyer was much higher than his subsequent rating as a President, correctly anticipated that the defense would rely on the Chase precedent. The Managers argued, therefore, that "abuse" and "usurpation" of judicial authority were sufficient to convict, that indictability was not required. The defense, headed by William Wirt, eminent libertarian lawyer and biographer of Patrick Henry, conceded that Peck had made an error but denied that he had committed a "high crime or misdemeanor" in the sense of the Constitution. "Even if the judge were proved to have mistaken the law," Wirt argued, "that would not warrant a conviction unless the guilt of intention be also established. For a mere mistake of the law is no crime or misdemeanor . . . It is the intention that is the essence of every crime." The Senate accepted Wirt's argument, and Peck was acquitted. This decision narrowed the definition of impeachability even further, to an intentionally committed indictable crime.

Thirty years passed before the House voted the next impeachment in 1862, against Judge West H. Humphreys of Tennessee. Humphreys had accepted a judgeship under the Confederacy without resigning from his United States post. Nominally, he had committed a form of treason. The definition of impeachability was not an issue in this case. Indeed, there was hardly any issue at all, as Humphreys offered no defense, either in person or by attorney. The charges included such offenses as refusing to hold court, organizing armed rebellion, and advocating and supporting secession. Humphreys could have been charged simply with treason, but the *prima facie* case was so strong that it made little difference whether he was impeached by a narrow or by a broad interpretation of impeachability. It was 1862, a civil war was on, and he was guilty either way.

In contrast, the next case resumed the pattern of narrow definition of impeachment. Not only was it the first impeachment of a President, but the acquittal of Andrew Johnson represented the greatest departure from the intent of the Framers of the Constitution relating to impeachment when enough Senators refused to vote for conviction of the President because they did not see intentional indictable criminal behavior. One cannot help but feel that had the meaning of the Founding Fathers not been misconstrued, Andrew Johnson would have been convicted.

The impeachment and trial of Andrew Johnson was a traumatic experience for Americans. (The summary at the end of this section gives the salient facts of the case and the Articles of Impeachment are reproduced in greater detail in the Appendix.) Some scholars have portrayed the whole proceeding as political persecution, perpetrated unnecessarily by fanatic anti-Johnson partisans. A widely accepted appraisal treats Johnson's acquittal as having repelled an "insidious assault" on our constitutional system by preserving the separation of powers and checks and balances in the American government and arresting misguided legislative tyranny. But that appraisal is clouded by a misconception of the nature and purpose of impeachment. Indeed, what Americans have been taught about the Johnson impeachment can hardly convince them of the soundness of this procedure to remove a despotic and tyrannical chief executive. Whatever wrongs Johnson may have committed, his impeachment and trial have been recorded as worse.

Events of Reconstruction which led to Johnson's impeachment are too numerous for a detailed recapitulation. Most Americans are familiar with Johnson's succession to the presidency in April, 1865, following the assassination of Abraham Lincoln, and his immediate assumption of the burden of restoring a war-torn nation. He intended to re-establish civil government in the former Confederate states as expeditiously as possible, with a minimal encroachment on Southern institutions, except for the abolition of slavery. A Union restored under this policy, he believed, would allow the scars of war to heal quickly and help eliminate the differences which had brought on the conflict. Throughout the war Lincoln had maintained that secession was illegal and theoretically never had occurred. Individuals may have rebelled, but states as political entities had never left the Union. Lawful governments had collapsed because rebellious Southerners allowed illegal Confederate governments to replace them. With rebel armies defeated, Southerners willing to support the United States could re-institute legal governments, and the Union would be restored. As Lincoln had before him, Johnson believed that the responsibility for restoration lay in the executive branch. Many disagreed, especially the powerful "Radical" wing of the Republican party. By the end of the war Radical leaders Thaddeus Stevens and Charles Sumner were speaking of "conquered provinces" and of "state suicide," asserting that "former" states no longer existed but had to be "re-constructed" and "re-admitted." And this, they insisted, was the Constitutional prerogative of Congress, not the executive. What had emerged was a conflict over legislative *versus* executive hegemony, whether Congress or the President should lead. One of the characteristics of the American system is a continuing struggle between the executive and legislative branches of our government for leadership and direction of national policy. It can be seen in many of the conflicts during the administrations of such "strong" Presidents as Thomas Jefferson, Andrew Jackson, Woodrow Wilson, and Franklin Roosevelt, although it emerged more clearly following World War II, and especially during the administration of Richard M.

Nixon. It was also a significant issue between Andrew Johnson and Congress.

There were other important differences. Congress and the President disagreed on the rights to be accorded the newly freed slaves; on tariff, agricultural, and industrial policies; and on the treatment of ex-Confederates. On a personal level, despite the fact that the Tennesseean was the only Southerner to remain in the Senate after secession, and despite his good record as a mayor, a state legislator, governor, senator, and military governor, Radicals scorned him as a Democrat and a Southerner. Johnson had grown up in poverty, and like Lincoln he epitomized the self-made man. Motherless at age three, he grew up as a tailor's apprentice, and not until he was eighteen did he learn to read and write. Where Lincoln stayed up nights reading lawbooks by flickering firelight, Johnson stayed up nights earning his living sewing by firelight. He hated "aristocrats" who snubbed him because of his humble background, and expressed this antagonism openly even after his political successes. After the South's defeat modified his views toward the planters, he extended his distaste to the war-rich industrialists who were associated with the new Republican party. "If Johnson were a snake," one of his opponents once observed acidly, "he would lie in the grass and bite the heels of rich men's children." Johnson also feared and mistrusted blacks, the competitors of the poor people from whom he had come. To ardent abolitionists who had viewed the Civil War as a crusade to gain freedom and equality for millions of degraded and oppressed fellow humans, Andrew Johnson was a "calamitous and traitorous Executive," "worse than Judas Iscariot or Benedict Arnold." Nor did Johnson's behavior as a campaigner help his image. He was a product of the backwoods hustings where stump-shouting invective, hard liquor, and rowdyism were common. Even after he was President, his origins showed through, as in the humiliating spectacle of his rough-and-ready campaign in 1866, the infamous "swing around the circle."

In one respect, the allegations of Johnson's detractors were grossly unfair. It is true that when he was inaugurated as Vice-President in 1865 he appeared to be drunk, but his weakness from a recent bout of typhoid fever had exaggerated the effect of a drink taken "to steady his nerves."

Whether his erratic inaugural behavior was primarily the result of liquor or illness is not certain, but he was never again publicly intoxicated. Nevertheless, this unfortunate episode was seized by his detractors to spread malicious gossip of habitual drunken debauchery.

Soon after becoming President, Johnson took steps to restore civil governments in the southern states. But his liberality toward white Southerners backfired. Former rebels gained political control in nearly every southern state. "Black codes" were legislated, reducing the freed blacks to a status of near-slavery. Unrepentant secessionists were returned to their former seats in Congress, giving Northerners reason to wonder whether the North or the South had won the war. Congressional Republicans reacted angrily. They refused to seat the southern Representatives and Senators, and took measures to enact their own program of Reconstruction. This opened the rift between Johnson and his party in Congress, a split which grew wider in the ensuing years and which led to the President's impeachment.

Traditional histories of the Reconstruction period have been sympathetic to neither Johnson nor the Radicals, though somewhat more apologetic for the President. He has been portrayed as honest and upright, but a poor and inept politician, anything but a giant among American political figures. The Radicals have fared worse. Portrayed as misguided patriots at best, they have more often been called fanatics, determined to make the South suffer for perpetrating slavery and the Civil War, insistent upon humiliating the white South and humbling the Presidency. In this view, the Radicals' hatred of Johnson was so great that they would go to any lengths to drive him out of office. Even if he did not merit impeachment, they would nevertheless interpret what he did as impeachable. On balance, traditional history has portrayed Johnson as the pathetic victim of a partisan Radical cabal.

Recent studies, perhaps influenced by the modern civil rights movement, view more favorably the intentions of the Radicals, but regret their "ill-directed passions." Indeed, Eric L. McKitrick questions whether the impeachment of Johnson was even necessary.[4] He points out that with their two-thirds control of both houses, Congressional Republicans were overriding Johnson's vetoes and effectively limiting his "usurpations." Furthermore, when impeachment was voted in 1868, Johnson had only one more year before his term expired. Rather than viewing the Radicals as fanatics, McKitrick and others describe them merely as impatient and unwise, and excuse the impeachment as an unfortunate and imprudent over-reaction.

Some scholars go further, and conclude that the portrayal of Johnson as the victim of aggressive and determined Radicals is entirely unfounded and erroneous. A recent study by Michael Benedict condemns the President, not the Radicals, as the perpetrator of immorality and injustice, and asserts that Johnson fully merited both impeachment and conviction.[5] Johnson was circumventing Congressional legislation and implementing his own programs through executive action. For example, his pardon of almost all Confederates included the return to them of their former lands, virtually wiping out crucial agrarian reforms Congress was trying to promote. Furthermore, Johnson unduly interfered in southern state affairs, using devious methods to prevent establishment of local governments under the terms of Congressional Reconstruction legislation. And finally, many Congressmen became convinced that Johnson even intended a military *coup* to enforce his own program of Reconstruction. His appointment of various generals into certain posts alarmed those who already mistrusted him, and his removal of Secretary of War Stanton provided the ultimate corroboration. Whereas a move to impeach Johnson in 1867 had found most Republicans reluctant to take that extreme step, by 1868 they had become convinced that the President's actions and intentions were subverting the Constitution. "The Johnson impeachment," concludes Benedict, "was the reluctant decision of men who had been pushed to the wall and forced to take a stand defending the constitutional prerogatives of Congress against presidential aggression."[6] Johnson's actions were no longer "light and transient"; they fully justified his removal.

Benedict argues also that traditional accounts of indiscretions and irregularities in the Senate trial are highly exaggerated. In spite of the firm control the Radicals had over the proceedings, Johnson's counsel was able to offer vital testimony which demolished the charge that the President deliberately plotted to violate the Constitution. Even though Senators delivered frequent and lengthy anti-Johnson harangues, defense counsel had ample opportunity to respond. Johnson's trial may have been the "best show in the nation," covered by reporters "like a murder case," but the impeachment and trial of a President are not everyday occurrences. Incidents such as that of a Washington woman who awakened a Congressman at midnight and refused to leave his house until he had promised to get her admitted to the Senate gallery should not discredit Radical Republicans struggling to preserve the Constitution.

A recent biography of Thaddeus Stevens injects another intriguing element into the Johnson impeachment — that it was a step toward parliamentary government.[7] Stevens considered the British system, with its stress on party solidarity, superior to the American. Americans could not change their governmental structure without a new Constitution, but the system could be improved by making the President more accountable. Stevens viewed Johnson impeachable primarily for betrayal of the Republican party. The Pennsylvania Congressman was not alone; others agreed that "high crimes and misdemeanors" should become a "convenient fiction" and impeachment "a piece of conventional political machinery" when the President no longer represented the will of the party. Impeachment, said the *New York Tribune*, "is not a mode of punishment, but a means of security and of avoiding political maladministration." This is reminiscent of sentiments expressed at the Constitutional Convention. Stevens had two criteria for impeachment: that the President no longer reflected his party, and that he had committed a legitimately impeachable offense. The first was no problem. But the second was, for in equating "legitimately impeachable offense" with an indictable crime, Stevens was a victim of the misconceived Chase doctrine. Then Johnson solved Stevens' problem by removing Secretary Stanton in violation of the Tenure of the Office Act.

From Stevens' point of view, the Johnson impeachment was the only process possible under the Constitution, other than waiting out the term — or violence — to maintain a viable political party structure. One might argue, of course, that the President was not only head of his party, he was also head of the country. This raises the obvious question: What if he no longer represented the will of the country?

According to Stevens the latter also constituted a legitimate reason for impeachment.

Views on the justification for President Johnson's impeachment and trial thus range between extremes. In the end, though, enough Senators were convinced that regardless of Johnson's administrative offenses, conviction for "high crimes and misdemeanors" required proof of intentional and indictable criminal action. "When the Constitution speaks of 'treason, bribery, and other high crimes and misdemeanors,'" argued Benjamin Robbins Curtis, former Supreme Court Justice and counsel for President Johnson, "it refers to and includes only high criminal offenses against the United States, made so by some law of the United States." Because it involved the President, the outcome of the Johnson impeachment represents the greatest departure from the intent of the Framers of the Constitution. Only by the narrow interpretation of high crimes and misdemeanors as it came from the misconceived Chase verdict could one-third of the Senators plus one justify their votes to acquit Andrew Johnson. By the original broader view of the Founding Fathers, he should have been convicted and removed from office.

The next impeachment involved William W. Belknap, Secretary of War in the Grant administration, accused of receiving kick-backs for lucrative civilian appointments on military posts. As in the Humphreys case, this impeachment and trial occurred in special circumstances which made it an exception to the 19th-century trend. Belknap resigned only hours before the House voted to impeach him, but his Senate trial proceeded anyway. The defense maintained that he was a private citizen no longer subject to impeachment; House Managers argued that Belknap's resignation was merely a ruse to escape punishment. Most Senators were convinced that Belknap was blatantly guilty of the corruption charges but his resignation prior to his formal impeachment suggested the possibility that convicting someone no longer a "civil officer" would be considered attainder — punishment by the legislature rather by than the courts — which is specifically prohibited by the Constitution. This jurisdictional question dominated the trial, and broad or narrow interpretations of high crimes and misdemeanors were not at issue. In the face of this Constitutional dilemma, the Senate acquitted Belknap.

Nearly three decades passed before the next impeachment hinted a return to the intent of the Framers of the Constitution. In 1903 District Judge Charles Swayne of Florida was charged with "high crimes and misdemeanors" committed both on and off the bench. Some of the charges against Swayne involved criminal offenses, yet neither House Managers nor defense counsel concentrated on them. Because of weak evidence, it was difficult to prove that the criminal offenses had actually been committed, and if committed, whether they were high crimes and misdemeanors. Counsel engaged in lengthly debates over the distinction, if any, between "personal crimes" committed off the bench and "official misconduct" on the bench. Swayne was acquitted, apparently from a combination of lack of evidence and Senatorial doubts about its jurisdiction over "personal crimes." Most significant, though, was the lack of emphasis upon criminal indictability.

A more important departure from the Chase Doctrine was soon to come. In 1912 Judge Robert W. Archbald of the United States Commerce Court was charged with a series of offenses including bribery, using his office for personal profit and political favors, and other examples of "misbehavior," "gross and improper conduct," and "high crimes and misdemeanors." Some of the offenses charged were criminal and therefore indictable, as House Managers John A. Sterling of Illinois and George W. Norris of Nebraska pointed out. The prosecution went far beyond the criminal charges, however, demonstrating that historically "high crimes and misdemeanors" emcompassed also non-criminal misconduct which could justify removal from office. On the other hand, the defense did not emphasize indictability, primarily because some of Archbald's actions were clearly indictable anyway — bribery, for instance. Indeed, Archbald readily admitted to the misdeeds, but he denied criminal intent, the argument used in the Peck case. For this reason the defense concentrated on the meaning of the Constitutional term "good behavior" as tenure for judges, and stressed that it must be distinguished from "pleasure of the Senate." They argued that there must be no doubt that the accused had committed high crimes and misdemeanors, no matter how tyrannical the individual or reprehensible his actions. To convict without proof of intent would be a subversion of the impeachment clause of the Constitution. The Senate found Judge Archbald guilty. For the first time since the Chase verdict in 1804, the Senate had resorted to the interpretation of impeachability intended by the Framers of the Constitution. Constitutional "high crimes and misdemeanors" again included non-criminal and non-indictable misuse of public office as well as indictable criminal offenses.

Three more impeachments followed the Archbald case, all strengthening the principle re-established there. In 1925 Judge George W. English of Illinois was charged with "showing favoritism" and with "arbitrary" and "tyrannical" conduct. English resigned before his trial could begin, and the House withdrew its charges, in spite of the precedent in the Belknap case. Some Congressmen objected that Judge English got off too easily, and argued strongly that his misdeeds merited conviction. But the majority agreed that even though English seemed blatantly guilty, the Senate could do no more than remove him from an office he had already surrendered. This did not satisfy fiery Representative Fiorello H. LaGuardia, who wanted the Senate to proceed with the trial so it would have "the opportunity of passing judicially on these unlawful, improper, and dishonest acts and so denounce them that no judge would ever have the temerity to repeat any of them." Even though the charges were dropped, the overwhelming original House vote for impeachment demonstrated that impeachable misconduct did not have to be criminal or indictable.

The English case poses an interesting side issue. Judge English knew that undoubtedly he would be convicted. He also knew that *all* the Senate could do was remove him from office. By resigning, he avoided trial and remained forever free of the non-criminal charges for which he was impeached. Might this set a precedent for future officials when they are impeached? Of course, if their offenses are criminal and indictable, they can still be brought into the regular courts after they are out of office. But if the offenses are non-criminal and non-indictable but still impeachable, and if the charges are dropped because the offender has resigned, he has avoided the further stigma of a Senate conviction. That has not yet occurred.

In 1932 Judge Harold Louderback of California was impeached for non-criminal actions amounting to favoritism and judicial imprudence. He was acquitted — not because his offenses were not impeachable, but because they could not be proved. Anticipating this, the House Judiciary Committee had recommended only censure, but the House impeached Louderback anyway. Even though he was acquitted, there was no longer any doubt that non-criminal improprieties and acts of misconduct were impeachable offenses.

Hardly had the Louderback case ended in 1933 when the House impeached Judge Halsted L. Ritter of Florida. Again the charges consisted of a variety of judicial improprieties on and off the bench, including income tax violations. The Senate vote fell just short of the required two-thirds for conviction on six of the charges, each listing a single offense. But Ritter was convicted on the seventh, a general charge that the cumulative impact of his indiscretions had brought the court "into scandal and disrepute, to the prejudice of . . . public confidence in the administration of justice therein, and to the prejudice of public respect for and confidence in" the workability of the federal court system. Senator Warren Austin of Vermont, who voted for acquittal, reacted critically that "the sum of six acquittals . . . [should not be] a conviction." "The necessary conclusion," he deplored, "is that a Federal judge has been removed from his office for general misbehavior not amounting to a crime."

Nearly four decades have passed since the Ritter conviction without further impeachments. Demands for impeachment have been heard often enough, but they have usually been dismissed by the public as political rhetoric. In the 1950's and 1960's "Impeach Earl Warren" on roadside billboards reflected a campaign to remove a liberal Chief Justice. Resolutions to impeach President Harry S Truman in 1952, Justice William O. Douglas in 1970, and President Richard M. Nixon in 1972 all died in the House Judiciary Committee for want of genuine impeachability. Thus in the almost two hundred years of the nation's history, only twelve times has the House of Representatives resorted to the Constitutional remedy of impeachment for oppression and misconduct amounting to "high crimes and misdemeanors." Other oppressive officials, some of them no doubt impeachable, were turned out by the voters, dismissed by higher officials, or pressured to resign. But when needed, impeachment was available. That it was not needed more often is a credit to the viability of the American political system. That it was not used more often may have been due to misconceptions about impeachability. Those no longer exist. Any future impeachment proceeding undoubtedly would be conducted within a frame of reference understandable to the Founding Fathers.

SUMMARY OF THE TWELVE AMERICAN IMPEACHMENTS

1. William Blount

Position: United States Senator from Tennessee
Date: 1797-1799
Description of Case: On April 21, 1797, Senator William Blount, former Commissioner of Indian Affairs, wrote to James Carey, a government interpreter to the Cherokee Nation, of his plans to organize Creek and Cherokee Indians and frontiersmen, aided by a British fleet, against Louisiana and Spanish Florida. England was at war with Spain; Blount's filibustering expedition would help England to gain control over those two areas. Carey turned the letter over to President John Adams. On July 3, 1797, Adams sent copies to both the House and the Senate, informing them of Blount's conspiracy.

In the Senate, Blount's letter was sent to a select committee which duly recommended his expulsion for "a high misdemeanor, entirely inconsistent with his public trust and duty as a Senator." The Senate expelled Blount on July 8, 1797, by a 25-1 vote.

In the House, meanwhile, a special committee had recommended that Blount be impeached. On July 7 the House approved that resolution, and on the same day appointed a committee to prepare formal articles of impeachment. Five articles were adopted on January 20, 1798. The trial in the Senate began on December 17, 1798; it concluded on January 11, 1799.

Summary of Charges: Article 1: Conspiring to carry on a military expedition against Spanish territory in violation of the laws and the obligations of neutrality of the United States.

Article 2: Conspiring to incite the Creek and Cherokee Indians to warfare in furtherance of the above mentioned scheme and in violation of the laws of the United States and of a treaty between the United States and Spain.

Article 3: Attempting to diminish and destroy the influence with the Creek and Cherokee Indian tribes of the principal Federal agent in the area against the laws of the United States.

Article 4: Attempting to "seduce" a Federal agent stationed at a trading post in the Cherokee Indian territories into assisting Blount in his "criminal intentions and conspiracies," against the laws and treaties of the United States.

Article 5: Attempting to impair the confidence of the Cherokee Indians in the United States and to "create and foment discontents and disaffection among said Indians" toward the United States.

Disposition: Acquitted of all charges on the ground that a United States Senator is not a "civil officer" of the United States as that term is used in impeachment clause of the Constitution.

2. John Pickering

Position: District Judge, District Court for the District of New Hampshire

Date: 1803-1804

Description of Case: On February 4, 1803, President Thomas Jefferson sent a complaint to the House of Representatives, citing Judge Pickering for irregular judicial procedures, loose morals, and drunkenness. The complaint was referred to a special committee, and on March 2, 1803, the House adopted that committee's resolution of impeachment. Not until October 20 was a committee appointed to prepare articles, but these were adopted by a voice vote on December 30. The trial began in the Senate on March 8, 1804, and lasted until March 12.

Summary of Charges: Article 1: In the course of proceedings by the United States to condemn a ship and its cargo for violation of custom laws, Judge Pickering delivered the ship to the claimant without requiring a bond, as required by law.

Article 2: In the same case, he refused to hear certain testimony offered by the government.

Article 3: In the same case, he refused to grant an appeal by the government, contrary to federal statute.

Article 4: "Being a man of loose morals and intemperate habits," he appeared on the bench on November 11 and 12, 1802, "in a state of intoxication ... and there frequently, in a most profane and indecent manner, [invoked] the name of the Supreme Being."

Disposition: Judge Pickering did not appear to defend himself, but his son, Jacob S. Pickering, testified that the judge had been insane and "wholly deranged" for at least two years, "incapable of corruption of judgment.... and his disorder has baffled all medical aid." Pickering was convicted by a vote of 19-7 on each of the four articles.

3. Samuel Chase

Position: Associate Justice, United States Supreme Court
Date: 1804-1805
Description of Case: On January 7, 1804, by an 81-40 vote, the House of Representatives adopted a resolution by John Randolph of Virginia calling for an investigation of Justice Chase and of District Judge Richard Peters for their conduct in the 1798 treason trial of John Fries. Fries had organized the farmers in western Pennsylvania to resist certain taxes, a protest reminiscent of the Whiskey Rebellion, but on a smaller scale. The House dropped action against Judge Peters by a voice vote on March 12, but on the same day, by a 73-32 vote, it adopted a resolution to impeach Justice Chase. Along with the Fries case, the House considered Chase's conduct in three other instances. One was the trial of James T. Callender, a Virginia printer accused under the Sedition Act. The others were grand jury hearings in Delaware and Maryland, also involving the Sedition Act. Formal articles were finally agreed to in a series of votes on December 4. The trial began in the Senate on February 9, 1805, and lasted until March 1.

Summary of Charges: Article 1: "Highly arbitrary, oppressive, and unjust" conduct at the trial of John Fries, delivering an opinion on a question of law before defendant's counsel had been heard, restricting defense counsel from citing English authorities and certain statutes of the United States on treason, and denying defendant's constitutional right to argue (through counsel) questions of law before the jury.

Articles 2-6: These dealt with the Callender case. Refusing to excuse a juror who had already made up his mind; refusing to allow a defense witness to testify; "manifest injustice, partiality, and intemperance" in compelling defense counsel to submit in writing questions to be asked a witness; "rude and contemptuous expressions" toward defense counsel; denial of bail in violation of the law; "repeated and vexatious interruptions" of defense counsel; and "an indecent solicitude . . . for the conviction of the accused . . . highly disgraceful to the character of a judge."

Article 7: Improperly attempting to induce a grand jury to indict a newspaper editor for violation of the sedition laws, and refusing to discharge grand jury when they refused to do so.

Article 8: Delivering to a grand jury "an intemperate and inflammatory political harangue, with intent to excite the fears and resentment of said grand jury and of the good people of Maryland against their State government and constitution . . . [in a manner] highly indecent, extra-judicial, and tending to prostitute the high judicial character with which he was invested to the low purpose of an electioneering partisan."

Disposition: Acquitted. The Senate failed to produce a two-thirds majority on any of the eight articles because no indictable crime could be proved. "Not guilty" outnumbered the "guilty" votes on five articles.

4. James H. Peck

Position: District Judge, District Court of Missouri

Date: 1826-1831

Description of Case: A land claims case decided by Judge Peck in 1826 resulted in such criticism that he published an article in a St. Louis newspaper explaining his decision. Luke E. Lawless, lawyer for the losing litigant, the socially prominent Soulard family, countered with another article listing eighteen legal errors in Peck's decision as well as other allegations about Peck's judicial behavior. In a very stormy court session, Judge Peck declared Lawless guilty of contempt, ordered him to prison for twenty-four hours, and suspended him from practicing in federal court for eighteen months. On December 8, 1826, Lawless wrote a "memorial" to the House of Representatives, detailing what he described as violation of speech and press freedoms, and requesting an investigation. The request died in the House Judiciary Committee. A similar petition in 1828 met the same fate. The reason was political; the status of western land grants had become a volatile issue in Congress. When the election of Andrew Jackson in 1828 changed the composition of Congress, a third "memorial" resulted in action. Following a Judiciary Committee investigation, on April 24, 1830, the House voted a resolution of impeachment, 123-49. A single Article was approved by a voice vote on May 1. The trial in the Senate began on December 20, 1830, and lasted until January 31, 1831.

Summary of Charges: Gross abuse of power as a judge in sentencing an attorney to twenty-four hours imprisonment and suspending him from the bar for eighteen months for writing and publishing a letter criticizing the judge's decision in a case in which the attorney had appeared.

Disposition: Acquitted, 21 Senators for conviction, 22 for acquittal, because criminal intent could not be proved. Among the prominent persons involved were James Buchanan, one of the House Managers, and Daniel Webster and William Wirt, defense counsel.

5. West H. Humphreys

Position: District Judge, District Court for the District of Tennessee

Date: 1862

Description of Case: During the Civil War, Judge Humphreys accepted an appointment as a Confederate judge without resigning from his United States judicial assignment. On January 8, 1862, by a voice vote, the House adopted a resolution authorizing the Judiciary Committee to investigate. It reported on May 6, and by another voice vote adopted a committee resolution impeaching Humphreys. Articles of Impeachment, drafted by a committee appointed May 14, were adopted by voice vote on May 19.

Summary of Charges: Article 1: Giving a public speech on December 29, 1861, declaring the right of secession.

Article 2: Unlawfully supporting and advocating the secession of Tennessee from the Union "along with other evil-minded persons."

Article 3: Unlawfully aiding in the organization of an armed rebellion and levying war against the United States.

Article 4: Conspiring to oppose the authority of the government of the United States by force contrary to the laws of the United States and his duty as judge.

Article 5: Refusing to hold court in his district as required by law.

Article 6: Unlawfully acting as judge of a Confederate court; and as judge of that court, requiring a man to swear allegiance to the Confederacy, ordering confiscation of property belonging to American citizens, and causing people to be arrested and imprisoned because of their allegiance to the United States.

Article 7: "Without lawful authority and with intent to injure," causing a citizen of the United States to be arrested and imprisoned.

Disposition: The trial lasted one day, June 26, 1862. Humphreys was convicted by a 38-0 vote.

6. Andrew Johnson

Position: President of the United States
Date: 1867-1868
Description of Case: First Attempt: Radical Republicans in Congress and President Johnson carried on a running battle over postwar Reconstruction programs. Some scholars have described Johnson's policies as conciliatory and lenient, Congress' as repressive. Others point to such aggressive Southern measures as "Black Codes," election of ex-Confederate leaders to positions of new leadership, and the determination of many Southerners to achieve through Reconstruction what they had failed to win either by secession or on the battlefield. Complicating the situation were inter- and intra-party squabbles as well as the persistent conflict of executive *versus* legislative prerogatives. Johnson's use of a number of executive devices, especially the veto, convinced many that the President was obstructing and by-passing important Congressional measures and preventing the implementation of necessary programs. At the same time, Radicals were also uncompromising and exceedingly severe in some of their attitudes. President Johnson carried these issues to the electorate in the mid-term elections of November, 1866. The outcome was a crushing defeat for him and an overwhelming victory for his opponents. On January 7, 1867, two Radical Republicans, Representatives James M. Ashley (Ohio) and Benjamin F. Loan (Missouri) introduced resolutions calling for Judiciary Committee investigations of possible impeachment of the President. The Committee spent almost a full year gathering testimony, much of it highly critical of the President, and by a 5-4 vote recommended impeachment. On December 7, 1867, however, the House turned down the Committee proposal, 57-108. One important reason for the close vote

in Committee and the rejection in the House was that the President was not alleged to have committed any specific crime.

Second Attempt: Relations between the President and Congress continued to be strained. Johnson vetoed a number of measures, only to have them overridden by Congress. The President also continued executive practices which counteracted or by-passed acts of Congress. In spite of the earlier failure to impeach, in January, 1868, the House by a 99-31 vote adopted a resolution authorizing the joint committee on Reconstruction to "inquire what combinations have been made or attempted to be made to obstruct the due execution of the laws." To help the committee, the House made available the impeachment evidence gathered by the Judiciary Committee in 1867.

Then on February 21, 1868, President Johnson dismissed Secretary of War Edwin M. Stanton, a leading Radical sympathizer, and appointed General Lorenzo Thomas in his place. The dismissal violated the Tenure of Office Act of March 2, 1867, which required Senate concurrence in the removal of certain officers, and which made violation of the act a "high misdemeanor." The day after Johnson dismissed Stanton, the joint committee on Reconstruction recommended impeachment; now the President had committed a crime. Two days later, on February 24, 1868, by a 126-74 vote, the House adopted an impeachment resolution by Representative John Covode (Pennsylvania), and appointed a committee to draw up formal charges. In a series of votes on March 2 and 3, eleven Articles were approved. The trial began in the Senate on March 30, and ended on May 26, 1868.

Summary of Charges: (See Appendix for detailed listing.)
Articles 1-8: These dealt with the attempted removal of Stanton. Each itemized a separate crime — "unlawfully" removing Stanton, "violating" the Constitution, acting "with intent" to violate the Constitution, "conspiring" to violate the Constitution, "unlawfully" appointing General Thomas to an office where no vacancy legally existed, and similar detailed offenses.
Article 9: Directing the military commander of the Department of Washington to take orders directly from the President, in violation of an act of Congress that they be issued through the General of the Army.
Article 10: Intending to set aside the authority of Congress; attempting to bring Congress into contempt and reproach by "intemperate, inflammatory, and scandalous harangues" which were highly critical of Congress; degrading the Presi-

dency "to the great scandal of all good citizens" and thereby being "guilty of a high misdemeanor in office."

Article 11: This is sometimes called the "omnibus article." It repeated in slightly different language the charges of the others, adding that Johnson also denied the validity and authority of certain Congressional measures because Congress represented "only part of the States."

Disposition: President Johnson did not appear to testify. His legal counsel was a team headed by Henry Stanbery, who had resigned as Attorney-General to lead the defense. Associated with him were Benjamin R. Curtis (formerly an Associate Justice on the United States Supreme Court), Jeremiah S. Black (formerly Attorney-General in the Buchanan administration), William M. Evarts (later Attorney-General in the Grant administration), Thomas A.R. Nelson (later a judge on the Tennessee supreme court), and William S. Groesbeck (former Congressman and eminent Ohio lawyer). House Managers were led by George S. Boutwell and Benjamin F. Butler (both of Massachusetts) and Thaddeus Stevens (Pennsylvania), and included John A. Bingham (Ohio), James F. Wilson (Iowa), Thomas Williams (Pennsylvania), and John A. Logan (Illinois).

After weeks of intense and acrimonious argument and testimony, the first test came on May 16, on Article XI, regarded by the Radicals as the most likely to produce a vote for conviction. With thirty-six "guiltys" needed for the necessary two-thirds, the vote fell one short, 35-19. Stunned by the setback, House Managers put off further action until May 26. During the ensuing ten days tremendous pressures were brought to bear, especially on the seven Republicans who had voted with the Democrats for acquittal — William P. Fessenden (Maine), James W. Grimes (Iowa), John B. Henderson (Missouri), Joseph S. Fowler (Tennessee), Lyman Trumbull (Illinois), Peter G. Van Winkle (West Virginia), and Edmund G. Ross (Kansas).

On May 26, 1868, the Senate voted on Articles II and III. The intense drama of that episode has since become almost legendary. By identical 35-19 votes Johnson was acquitted on both articles. Recognizing the futility of balloting on the other articles, the Radicals promptly adjourned the proceedings *sine die.*

7. William W. Belknap

Position: Secretary of War
Date: 1876
Description of Case: Aroused by charges of widespread corruption and incompetence among high officials in the

Grant administration, the House on January 14, 1876, adopted by voice vote a resolution authorizing various committees to conduct investigations. Subsequently the Committee on Expenditures in the War Department reported major improprieties on the part of Secretary of War Belknap and recommended his impeachment. This was acceded to on March 2, 1876, by a voice vote of the House. Only hours earlier, though, President Grant had accepted Belknap's resignation. Nevertheless, the Judiciary Committee drew up five Articles of Impeachment, which were approved by the House on April 3. Considerable debate ensued in the Senate over the issue of jurisdiction, since Belknap had resigned prior to being impeached. On May 29 the Senate decided, 37-29, that it did have jurisdiction, and the trial was set.

Summary of Charges: All five articles dealt with graft involving the post-trader of Fort Sill, Oklahoma (John S. Evans), a middleman influence peddler (Caleb R. Marsh), and Belknap. In return for obtaining the very lucrative appointment, Evans periodically paid Marsh approximately $12,000 annually over a period of several years, of which Marsh paid off Belknap approximately $6,000 each year.

Disposition: The trial ran from July 6 to August 1, 1876. A majority of the Senators voted "guilty" on each count, but since it was short of the required two-thirds, Belknap was acquitted. Many Senators stated later that they voted for acquittal because they still doubted jurisdiction, Belknap having resigned earlier. They feared that if the Senate convicted Belknap, it would be tantamount to a bill of attainder, specifically prohibited by the Constitution.

8. Charles Swayne

Position: District Judge, District Court for the Northern District of Florida

Date: 1903-1905

Description of Case: Responding to requests of some of his constituents, Representative William B. Lamar (Florida) ascertained that Judge Swayne had taken undue personal advantage of his judicial post and had also dealt improperly with some attorneys who practiced in his court. On December 10, 1903, Lamar introduced a resolution, adopted by voice vote, for a Judiciary Committee investigation of Judge Swayne. The committee duly recommended impeachment, and on December 13, 1904, the House by voice vote approved the resolution. Twelve formal articles were

approved a month later, on January 18, 1905.
Summary of Charges: Articles 1-3: Making various false and fraudulent expense account claims against the government. *Articles 4-5:* Appropriating for his own use, without compensating the owner, a railroad car belonging to a railroad company in the hands of a receiver whom he had appointed.
Articles 6-7: Violating for six years a federal statute requiring a district judge to live within his judicial district.
Articles 8-12: "Maliciously and unlawfully" adjudging three lawyers in contempt of court and imposing on them unwarranted fines and prison sentences.
Disposition: The trial ran from February 10-27, 1905. The substantive evidence against Judge Swayne was very weak, and many observers were not surprised at a majority vote of "not guilty" on each article. Judge Swayne was therefore duly acquitted.

9. Robert W. Archbald

Position: Circuit Judge, United States Court of Appeals for the Third Circuit, serving as Associate Judge of the United States Commerce Court
Date: 1912-1913
Description of Case: Judge Archbald served on the United States District Court for the Middle District of Pennsylvania, and then was appointed Circuit Judge of the Third Judicial Circuit. In the latter capacity, he was also assigned to the United States Commerce Court. There he committed a number of indiscretions which resulted in a House Judiciary Committee investigation. On July 11, 1912, by an overwhelming 223-1 vote, the House adopted the committee's resolution for impeachment, which included thirteen articles of alleged improprieties. The trial in the Senate began on December 3, 1912, and concluded on January 13, 1913.
Summary of Charges: Articles 1-6 listed specific improprieties and misconduct while Judge Archbald was on the Commerce Court; Articles 7-12 detailed offenses committed earlier while on the District Court. Article 13 was a general listing of offenses committed on both.
Articles 1-6: Using his position to influence the sale price of a coal dump which he purchased, the seller being a litigant before him; "gross and improper conduct" in favoring an attorney in a case before him by communicating secretly to receive certain information after the completion of the

trial; accepting money from one railroad company for his support in its litigation with another railroad over the transfer of coal leases in which the judge had an interest; accepting money to intervene in cases before the Interstate Commerce Commission; speculating in culm bank (coal dump) properties of companies in litigation in his court.

Articles 7-12: Accepting financial and other favors from companies engaged in various litigations before him; participating in an investment, in a manner particularly advantageous to himself, with the owner of a company in litigation before him; improperly influencing a party in a litigation before him; accepting financial favors from lawyers in litigation before him.

Article 13: Obtaining credit from and through persons in litigation before him; attempting to influence litigations before the Interstate Commerce Commission for a financial consideration; using his influence and position to induce various railroads to enter into business contracts from which he profited; using his position to influence speculative business ventures for his own profit.

Disposition: Judge Archbald was convicted on Articles 1, 3, 4, and 5 dealing with specific misconduct on the Commerce Court, and on Article 13 dealing more generally with offenses committed on both the Commerce Court and the District Court. He was removed from the Bench and disqualified from further office.

10. George W. English

Position: District Judge, District Court for the Eastern District of Illinois

Date: 1925-1926

Description of Case: During the summer of 1922 the *East St. Louis* (Illinois) *Journal* and the *St. Louis Post-Dispatch* published a series of articles denouncing the disbarment by Judge English of Charles A. Karch, a lawyer practicing in English's court. The judge summoned the reporters into court and threatened them with imprisonment if they continued to publish such stories. Refusing to be intimidated, the *St. Louis Post-Dispatch* exposed several more instances of English's misconduct amounting virtually to a bankruptcy ring. Accordingly, on January 13, 1925, Representative Harry B. Hawes of Missouri introduced into the House of Representatives a resolution calling for an investigation. The House Judiciary Committee duly reported a resolution calling for the impeachment of Judge English, adopted by the House on April 1, 1926, by a 306-62 vote. Included in the resolution were five articles charging English with partiality and judicial tyranny and oppression. The Senate trial was set for November 10, 1926, but on November 4 English suddenly resigned.

Summary of Charges: Article 1: Suspending and disbarring several attorneys without charges being preferred against them, without prior notice, and without permitting them to defend themselves; summoning state attorneys and state sheriffs to appear in an imaginary and fictitious case and then denouncing them in open court in abusive and profane language; attempting to coerce jurymen by stating in open court that a defendant was guilty, and publicly threatening the jury if they did not find him so; summoning members of the press to appear in court and threatening them with imprisonment if they did not suppress publication of information about a particular disbarment proceeding.

Articles 2-3: Showing favoritism to a particular referee in a bankruptcy proceeding, to the personal profit of both himself and the referee; amending the rules of bankruptcy in his court to make the preceding possible.

Article 4: Directing that certain bankruptcy funds be deposited in banks in which he had an interest; securing employment for his son with certain banks by ordering bankruptcy funds placed in those banks, and in one instance with the interest to be paid to his son; borrowing funds with low or no interest charges from banks into which he directed bankruptcy funds be deposited.

Article 5: Mistreating members of the bar appearing in his court by arbitrary and tyrannical conduct; denying litigants the right to have counsel; denying defendants in criminal cases the right to trial by jury; showing favoritism toward certain bankruptcy referees; attempting to make a deal with a fellow judge whereby each would choose a particular relative of the other for certain receiverships and other appointments.

Disposition: After Judge English resigned, the House Managers recommended that the proceedings be discontinued. The earlier investigation leading to the House impeachment had convinced many that English was blatantly guilty (though only a Senate trial could legally declare him so). The Managers felt, however, that the Constitutional outcome (removal) had already been achieved since English was no longer on the bench. Many in both houses felt that English should not get off that easily, but it was agreed that too much time and public money would be spent for no apparently worthwhile purpose. The Senate was then engaged in such weighty issues as prohibition legislation and Muscle Shoals, and there was every expectation that Judge English would engage in many devious strategems to drag out his trial in order to escape punishment. Some argued that the Senate no longer had jurisdiction anyway, but the Belknap case was pointed out as a precedent that a trial could occur even though English was no longer a "civil officer." Nevertheless, the attitude prevailed that Judge English had already been branded as so despicable a judge that the Senate could spend its time more profitably on other pressing affairs. On December 11, 1926, by a 290-23 vote, the House requested the Senate to drop the case, and two days later, by a 70-9 vote, the Senate acceded.

11. Harold Louderback

Position: District Judge, District Court for the Northern District of California
Date: 1932-1933
Description of Case: On June 9, 1932, Representative Fiorello H. LaGuardia of New York introduced a resolution calling for an investigation of alleged judicial improprieties committed by Judge Louderback in bankruptcy and receivership proceedings. The resolution was adopted by a voice vote. The Judiciary Committee investigation produced mixed results. The majority recommended censuring rather than impeaching Louderback, there being sufficient evidence for the former but not for the latter. However, Congressman LaGuardia's minority resolution calling for impeachment was approved by the House after considerable discussion, on February 24, 1933, by a vote of 183-142. The resolution included five formal Articles of Impeachment. The trial began in the Senate on May 15, 1933.
Summary of Charges: The five articles alleged "tyranny and oppression, favoritism and conspiracy, whereby he has brought the administration of justice . . . into disrepute" in appointing certain bankruptcy receivers; granting "exorbitant" allowances to some receivers and attorneys who were "personal and political friends and associates" and "displaying a high degree of indifference" to others; conduct on the bench such as "to excite fear and distrust and to inspire a widespread belief . . . that causes were not decided in said court according to their merits, but were decided with partiality and with prejudice and favoritism . . . all of which is prejudicial to the dignity of the judiciary . . . to the

scandal and disrepute of said court and the administration of justice therein.''

Disposition: The trial in the Senate lasted from May 15 to May 24, 1933. On only one article did a majority vote "guilty"; on all others the "not guilty" votes outnumbered the "guilty." Apparently the majority of the House Judiciary Committee had surmised correctly that there was sufficient evidence to censure but not enough to convict Accordingly, Judge Louderback was acquitted.

12. Halsted L. Ritter

Position: District Judge, District Court for the Southern District of Florida

Date: 1933-1936

Description of Case: On May 29, 1933, Representative J. Mark Wilcox of Florida requested the House of Representatives to investigate alleged improprieties committed by Judge Ritter during the preceding four years. That resolution was adopted by a voice vote on June 1. The House Judiciary Committee investigation dragged on for almost three years, until it reported a resolution recommending impeachment. That resolution was adopted by the House on March 2, 1936, by a 181-146 vote. It included four formal Articles of Impeachment, three dealing with specific misdeeds allegedly committed, and a general article that was the sum of the first three. On March 30, before the trial in the Senate began, the articles were amended by House Resolution 471 (74th Congress, 2nd Session), adding three more specific charges and enlarging the last general article. The trial began in the Senate on April 6, 1936.

Summary of Charges: Articles 1-2: These were in the original charges. Conspiring in a champertous suit and corruptly and unlawfully receiving $4,500 from a former law partner whom Ritter had appointed as receiver in a bankruptcy case. The receiver's fee had been set originally by another judge at $15,000; Ritter raised it to $75,000.

Articles 3-4: These together had comprised the original Article 3; they were now separated. Engaging in the private practice of law while on the bench, in violation of federal law, and receiving fees for this illegal practice.

Articles 5-6: These were added to the original articles. Failure to pay income tax on $12,000 for 1929 and on $5,300 for 1930, the incomes referred to in Articles 1-4.

Article 7: By committing the "high crimes and misdemeanors" detailed in Articles 1-6, "the reasonable and

probable consequence of the actions or conduct of Halsted L. Ritter . . . as an individual or as such judge, is to bring his court into scandal and disrepute, to the prejudice of said court and public confidence in the administration of justice therein, and to the prejudice of public respect for and confidence in the Federal judiciary and to render him unfit to continue to serve as such judge. . . . Wherefore, the said Judge Halsted L. Ritter was and is guilty of misbehavior, and was and is guilty of high crimes and misdemeanors."
Disposition: The trial in the Senate lasted from April 6 to April 17. There were more "guilty" than "not guilty" votes on all except one of the first six specific articles, but these majorities all fell short of the two-thirds required for conviction. On the seventh article, however, with 56 votes required for conviction, the vote was 56-28. Thus Ritter was convicted and removed from office.

[1] A thirteenth, United States District Judge Mark Delahay, was impeached by the House in 1873, but the case was dropped before articles of impeachment were drawn up. Those cases not resulting in impeachment were disposed of in various ways. In most instances the person under inquiry resigned, resulting in the proceedings being discontinued. In some instances the investigatory committee either filed a report recommending against impeachment or dropped the investigation without even filing a report. In other instances the committee recommended censure rather than impeachment. Paul S. Fenton, "The Scope of the Impeachment Power," in *Impeachment — Selected Materials*, 663.

[2] Irving Brant, *Impeachment: Trials and Errors* (New York, 1972), 24-45.

[3] Raoul Berger, *Impeachment: The Constitutional Problems* (Cambridge, 1973), 224.

[4] Eric L. McKitrick, *Andrew Johnson and Reconstruction* (Chicago, 1960), 486-491.

[5] Michael Les Benedict, *The Impeachment and Trial of Andrew Johnson* (New York, 1973).

[6] Michael Les Benedict, "A New Look at the Impeachment of Andrew Johnson," *Political Science Quarterly*, LXXXVIII (September, 1973), 349.

[7] Fawn M. Brodie, *Thaddeus Stevens: Scourge of the South* (New York, 1959), 337-338.

3

Impeachable Offenses

THERE SHOULD no longer be any doubt about the fundamental nature of impeachment. It is a political, not a criminal, procedure, to remove government officials who commit either non-criminal or criminal wrongs. In the early 1800's impeachability had been narrowed by the Chase doctrine of criminal indictability which prevailed throughout the nineteenth century. Then in 1913 the original construction was restored by the Archbald decision. Political misconduct and abuses need not be tolerated because they are not indictable crimes. The obstruction which clouded the impeachment of President Andrew Johnson has been removed.

But another still exists. Put simply, it is the definition of "non-criminal offense." Where is the line which separates genuinely impeachable political evils from retributive personal or political partisanship? Those who argue that Andrew Johnson misused presidential powers and should have been convicted must concede that partisanship was a significant factor in his impeachment. One has only to examine Article X of the charges against Johnson to learn that hard-hitting political oratory can be an impeachable offense — when the orator is an official you are determined to remove from office! In the Federalist-Republican disputes of earlier years, even moderate Jeffersonians believed impeachment to be a proper political instrument to remove errant judges. Was it a coincidence, though, that the "errant" judges were Federalists, and were defended by Federalist lawyers such as Luther Martin and Joseph Hopkinson? In that era of fierce partisanship, Hopkinson stood out as a staunch party-line Federalist. Luther Martin, who "knew more law and could hold more brandy than anyone in

Maryland," hated Jefferson so intensely that his worst condemnation was to call someone "as great a scoundrel as Tom Jefferson." This is not to imply that the Johnson, Chase, and other impeachments lacked justification. On the contrary, there was considerable substantive cause for each of them. The dilemma is the degree of partisan and personal animosity involved in the interpretation of that substance.

This emphasis upon partisanship appears to impugn the character and integrity of Luther Martin, Joseph Hopkinson, Thaddeus Stevens, Charles Sumner, John Sterling, George Norris, and their counterparts in the twelve impeachment trials. Luther Martin, for instance, had attended the Constitutional Convention and knew the intent of the Framers; yet he and Joseph Hopkinson (whose father had been a delegate) interjected into the Chase trial the doctrine of criminal indictability which clearly contravened that intent. Did knowledgeable and reputable lawyers and legislators deliberately distort events and the law to suit their personal or political biases? Not if one recalls Thomas Macaulay's discerning aphorism: "We do not blame the accused and his counsel for availing themselves of every legal advantage in order to obtain an acquittal."

Reasonable persons disagree legitimately in their interpretations of events, law, and principles. And reasonable persons disagree on what is impeachable and what is not. This monumental dilemma was noted by Senator Samuel White of Delaware in the Pickering case, when he remarked that "good behavior" might be subverted to mere "pleasure of the Senate." That was precisely what the Framers had hoped to prevent when they rejected the ambiguities of "mal-practice" and "corruption" and "mal-administration" for the more precise and limited "high crimes and misdemeanors." The Pickering conviction, White warned, could set a precedent that "every officer of the Government must be at the mercy of a majority of Congress, and it will not hereafter be necessary that a man should be guilty of high crimes and misdemeanors . . ., but a conviction upon any facts stated in articles exhibited against him will be sufficient." The Chase doctrine removed that danger by its insistence upon criminal indictability. The "pleasure of the Senate" may have come close in the Johnson case, but still it did not degenerate into the disastrous vilification that Senator White had feared. Indeed, the narrowly-won acquittal of Andrew Johnson prevented the revival of that danger for more than four decades.

Then came the Archbald conviction, restoring non-criminal offenses to impeachability, but also reviving the problem that Senator White had envisioned. In an address before the American Bar Association in 1913, William Howard Taft pointed out: "By the liberal interpretation of the term 'high misdemeanors' which the Senate has given, there is now no difficulty in securing the removal of a judge for *any reason* that shows him unfit." [Author's italics.] Taft's assessment of the Archbald decision was verified and further defined by the House of Representatives when it impeached Judge George W. English in 1926:

It is now, we believe, considered that impeachment is not confined alone to acts which are forbidden by the Constitution or Federal statutes. The better sustained and modern view is that the provision for impeachment in the Constitution applies not only to high crimes and misdemeanors as those words were understood at common law but also acts which are not defined as criminal and made subject to indictment, and also to those which affect the public welfare. Thus an official may be impeached for offenses of a political character and for gross betrayal of public interests. Also for abuses or betrayal of trusts, for inexcusable negligence of duty, for the tyrannical abuse of power, . . . or for abuse or reckless exercise of discretionary power as well as the breach of an official duty imposed by statute or common law.

Making unbiased political decisions is extremely difficult under any circumstances; this broad definition magnifies it in determining impeachability. For instance, is an act or policy of a President that departs radically from the past, or that offends deep political, economic, or moral convictions, a "tyrannical abuse of power?" Were President Lyndon Johnson's and President Nixon's war policies in southeast Asia impeachable? If so, did they violate the Constitution and overstep their authority tyrannically and abusively, or did they simply persist in a war that violated moral convictions or controversial concepts of national interest? Those who reject war as "an instrument of national policy" see "tyranny" and "abuse" where those who favor a worldwide military presence do not. This is not to say that one is right and the other is wrong. On the contrary, both are right, but from their own point of view, and in the American scheme of things both are free to follow their own convictions. But consideration of impeachment demands that partisanship and personal conviction be suppressed in favor of attempting an objective determination of the nature of the abuse of power, and that is not easy to do. Recent history abounds in examples of national soul-searching over Presidential actions. Was Woodrow Wilson's advocacy of American membership in the League of Nations a "gross betrayal of public interest?" Was Lyndon Johnson's "Great Society" a perversion of the "public welfare?" Was Dwight Eisenhower's use of federal troops to enforce school integration "tyrannical abuse" and "reckless exercise of discretionary power?" Do the revelations which have emerged from the Watergate investigations constitute a "gross betrayal of public trust" by Richard M. Nixon? While these questions are not suggested as parallels, individuals, depending upon their frames of reference, have developed totally different conceptions of each situation.

Evaluation of possible impeachment offenses demands objectivity, impartiality, self-discipline, and serious consideration of alternatives. Impeachment is a grave matter under any circumstances, the more so when the accused is the President of the United States. Impeachment investigators must rely upon sound interpretations of precedents and reputable legal authority; even then interpretations will differ. Two valuable sources of such information are *Hinds' Precedents of the House of Representatives* and *Cannon's Precedents of the House of Representatives*. Former Congressmen Asher Crosby Hinds and Clarence Cannon were experts in parliamentary practice and procedure. Their lengthy analyses, arguments, and rulings are the major compilations of impeachment precedent and law. Representative selections from their works are found on page 72 and page 85.

Talk of impeaching controversial officials has been almost commonplace political rhetoric during the turbulent years since Judge Ritter was removed in 1936, but the best-organized effort occurred in 1970 with the move to impeach Associate Justice William O. Douglas of the United States Supreme Court. For more than three decades Douglas had championed civil rights and civil liberties both on and off the bench, and had become a prime target for those with differing political philosophies. After President Nixon's nominations of Clement Haynsworth and G. Harrold Carswell for the Supreme Court were rejected by the Senate, a counter-current of frustration and resentment focused on Douglas. On April 15, 1970, Representative Andrew Jacobs of Indiana introduced an impeachment resolution on the floor of the House of Representatives. The House Judiciary Committee conducted a thorough investigation, and later that year dismissed all charges. The controversy and investigation precipitated and updated research on impeachment, and the arguments presented on both sides represent the most recent views of the boundaries of impeachability.

Minority Floor Leader Gerald R. Ford of Michigan, later the first Vice-President chosen under the Twenty-fifth Amendment, made a succinct statement of his position on impeachment and removal. Speaking in favor of impeaching Douglas, Ford endorsed the Archbald decision and the broad positions suggested by William Howard Taft and the House charges against Judge English. After mentioning historic differences about impeachability, Ford declared that now, at least, "authorities can agree . . . that an offense need not be indictable to be impeachable," and that an offender could be removed for "something less than a criminal act or criminal dereliction of duty." "What, then, is an impeachable offense?" rhetorically asked Congressman Ford. "The only honest answer is that an impeachable offense is whatever a majority of the House of Representatives considers [it] to be at a given moment in history; conviction results from whatever offense or offenses two-thirds of the other body considers to be sufficiently serious to require removal of the accused from office."

Ford's speech in the House of Representatives was widely publicized, but equally important were the arguments filed by opposing counsel with a special subcommittee of the House Judiciary Committee. At the request of Congressman Ford, constitutional lawyers Bethel B. Kelley and Daniel G. Wyllie prepared a legal memorandum supporting the impeachment of Douglas through a broad definition of impeachability. The "conscience of Congress," concluded the Kelley Memorandum (see page 91), should determine the nature of misbehavior requiring impeachment and removal from office.

In contrast, a statement filed with the subcommittee by Douglas' counsel, Simon H. Rifkind, argued for a much narrower definition (see page 93). Judge Rifkind conveniently returned to the Chase doctrine, that "impeachment is for criminal offenses only." Historically, his argument was exceedingly weak; Raoul Berger has generously referred to it as "so strange a construction on Senate precedents."

The Douglas case stands as a classic example of the misuse of impeachment. Ostensibly Douglas was charged with "high crimes and misdemeanors" such as accepting fees for speeches and consulting services, for alleged income tax discrepancies, and for writing inflammatory materials labelled revolutionary. In reality, the major factor behind the charges was Douglas' judicial liberalism, the very partisan abuse that Senator White and William Howard Taft had feared. Ironically, the fundamental position of his accusers on impeachability had much more merit than those of his defenders. Had the charges against Douglas been genuinely impeachable, undoubtedly he would have been removed. But the dismissal of the case reenforced the doctrine that impeachability stemming from ideological differences and factional partisanship is not valid. The warnings of White and Taft have been heeded.

Then, on July 31, 1973, a resolution calling for the impeachment of President Richard M. Nixon was introduced on the floor of the House of Representatives. Speaking for the resolution, Representative Robert F. Drinan of Massachusetts gave an up-to-date summary of presidential "activities or omissions" which constitute impeachable conduct (see page 105). As Gerald Ford had in 1970, Drinan argued that impeachment is a legitimate recourse to curb a chief executive's misconduct which is "less than criminal but more than tolerable."

HINDS' PRECEDENTS

Before being elected Representative from Maine in 1910, Asher Crosby Hinds served for twenty-two years in the office of the Speaker of the House. He was editor of *Rules, Manual, and Digest of the House of Representatives* (1899) and of the monumental *Hinds' Precedents of the House of Representatives* (1907). In addition to rulings and decisions of Speakers and chairmen of the Committee of the Whole, these outstanding parliamentary works also contain analyses, arguments, and rulings in impeachment litigations. Together with *Cannon's Precedents* they constitute the foremost authority on Congressional practice and impeachment precedents. The following selections are excerpts from the chapter that deals with impeachment. The full text of this portion of *Hinds' Precedents* is reprinted in *Impeachment — Selected Materials*, 27-87.

2008. Reference to discussions as to what are impeachable offenses.

In the course of the arguments during the impeachment trial of Andrew Johnson, President of the United States, the question, "What are impeachable offenses?" was discussed at length and learnedly. Mr. Manager Benjamin F. Butler, of Massachusetts, argued learnedly in favor of this definition:

> We define therefore an impeachable high crime or misdemeanor to be one in its nature or consequences subversive of some fundamental or essential principle of government or highly prejudicial to the public interest, and this may consist of a violation of the Constitution, of law, of an official oath, or of duty, by an act committed or omitted, or, without violating a positive law, by the abuse of discretionary powers from improper motives or for any improper purpose.

Mr. Butler also appended to his argument an exhaustive brief on the "law of impeachable crimes and misdemeanors," prepared by Mr. William Lawrence, of Ohio. This view was also supported by Mr. Manager John A. Logan, of Illinois. Of the Senators who filed written opinions, Mr. Charles Sumner, of Massachusetts, argued at length that political offenses were impeachable offenses. So also argued Mr. Richard Yates, of Illinois.

Mr. Benjamin R. Curtis, of Massachusetts, of counsel for the President, argued, on the other hand, that impeachable offenses could only be offenses against the laws of the United States. Mr. Thomas A. R. Nelson, of Tennessee, also of President's counsel, argued in the same line, and Mr. William M. Evarts, of New York, also of counsel for the President, argued at length against the definition given by Mr. Manager Butler. Of the Senators who filed written opinions on the case, this view was sustained by Mr. Garrett Davis, of Kentucky.

2009. Argument that the phrase "high crimes and mis-demeanors" is a "term of art," of fixed meaning in English parliamentary law, and transplanted to the Constitution in unchangeable significance.

I. WHAT ARE IMPEACHABLE "HIGH CRIMES AND MISDE-MEANORS," AS DEFINED IN ARTICLE II, SECTION 4, OF THE CONSTITUTION OF THE UNITED STATES?

By a strange coincidence, the death of parliamentary impeachment, as a living and working organ of the English constitution, synchronizes with its birth in American constitutions, State and Federal. Leaving out of view the comparatively unimportant impeachment of Lord Melville (1805), really the last of that long series of accusations by the Commons and trials by the Lords, which began in the fiftieth year of the reign of Edward III (1376), was the case of Warren Hastings, who was impeached in the very year in which the Federal Convention of 1787 met at Philadelphia. Before that famous prosecution, with its failure and disappointment, drew to a close, the English people resolved that the ancient and cumbrous machinery of parliamentary impeachment was no longer adapted to the wants of a modern and progressive society. But before this ancient method of trial thus passed into desuetude in the land of its birth it was embodied, in a modified form, first in the several State constitutions and finally in the Constitution of the United States. . . .

II. PROVISIONS BORROWED FROM THE ENGLISH CONSTITUTION

. . . "If we examine the clauses of the Constitution, we perceive at once that the phraseology is applied to a method of procedure already existing. 'Impeachment' is not defined, but is used precisely as 'felony,' 'larceny,' 'burglary,' 'grand jury,' 'real actions,' or any other legal term used so long as to have acquired an accepted meaning, might be. The Constitution takes impeachment as an established procedure, and lodges the jurisdiction in a particular court, declaring how and by whom the process shall be put in motion, and how far it shall be carried. They have given to us a thing not of their creation, but of their modification. To ascertain, then, what this established procedure was, what were, at the time of the Constitutional Convention, impeachable offenses, we must look to England, where the legal notion contained in the clauses quoted had their origin." . . .

III. HIGH CRIMES AND MISDEMEANORS AS DEFINED IN ENGLISH PARLIAMENTARY LAW

. . . It has always been conceded that the phrase "other high crimes and misdemeanors," embodied in Article II, section 4, of the Constitution of the United States, must be construed in the light of the definitions fixing its meaning in the parliamentary law of England as that law existed in 1787. The construction then given to the phrase in question was incorporated into our Federal Constitution as a part of the phrase itself, which is unintelligible and meaningless without such construction. . . .

While the Senate sitting as a court of impeachment is the sole and final judge of what impeachable "high crimes and misdemeanors" are, no arbitrary discretion so to determine is vested. The power of the court simply extends to the construction of the phrase in question as defined in English constitutional and parliamentary law as it existed in 1787. That is made plain by Story in his Commentary on the Constitution, section 797, when he says: "Resort then must be had either to parliamentary practice, and the common law, in order to ascertain what high crimes and misdemeanors: or the whole subject must be left to the arbitrary discretion of the Senate for the time being. The latter is so incompatible with the genius of our institutions that no lawyer or statesman would be inclined to countenance so absolute a despotism of opinion and practice, which might make that a crime at one time or in one person which would be deemed innocent at another time or in another person. The only safe guide in such cases must be the common law."

IV. A RULE OF CONSTITUTIONAL CONSTRUCTION AS DEFINED BY THE SUPREME COURT OF THE UNITED STATES

The fundamental principles of English constitutional law were first reproduced in the constitutions of the several States. In the light of the construction put upon them there, they were embodied, so far as applicable and desirable, in the Constitution of the United States. Thus the Federal Supreme Court was called upon at an early day to interpret the immemorial formulas or "terms of art" through which the cardinal principles of English constitutional law were incorporated in our governmental systems, State and Federal. The uniform rule for construing such formulas or "terms of art" adopted at the outset has been continued in force until the present time. . . .

V. IMMEMORIAL FORMULAS TRANSPLANTED FROM THE ENGLISH CONSTITUTION, UNCHANGEABLE BY SUBSEQUENT CONGRESSIONAL LEGISLATION

The foregoing authorities put the fact beyond all question that the immemorial formulas or "terms of art" transferred from the English constitution to our own were adopted, not as isolated or abstract phrases, but as epitomes or digests of the great principles which they embodied. . . . In other words, when such formulas were embedded in the Constitution of 1787, their historical meaning and construction went along with them as completely as if such meaning and construction had been written out at length upon the face of the instrument itself. If that be true, the conclusion is self-evident that no subsequent Congressional legislation can change in any way, by addition or subtraction, the definitions embodied in such formulas at the time of their adoption. If the contrary were true, Congress could any day give to the term "levying war" or "due process of law" a definition, conveying ideas of which the fathers never dreamed. Or if the term "high crimes and misdemeanors" could be subjected to a new Congressional definition, acts which were such in 1787 could be relieved of all criminality, and new acts not then criminal could be added to the list of impeachable offenses. So obvious is that case that Congress can not legislate at all on the subject. . . .

If Congress could, by subsequent legislation, "define or limit by law that which the Constitution defines," the Senate sitting as a court of impeachment could be entirely deprived by such legislation of the power to determine what were impeachable high crimes and misdemeanors as defined by the fathers in 1787. In other words, if Congress can add to or subtract from the constitutional definition in any particular, it can destroy it altogether. In the great case of Marbury *v.* Madison (1 Cranch 137) the first in which an act of Congress was ever declared unconstitutional, the question of questions was this: Does the fact that the Constitution itself has defined the original jurisdiction of the Supreme Court prohibit Congress from enlarging such original jurisdiction by subsequent legislation? The solemn answer was that the attempt of Congress to do so was void. Why? Because the dividing line between the original and appellate jurisdiction having been drawn by the Constitution itself, it is immovable by legislation. In the words of the great Chief Justice: "If Congress remains at liberty to give this court appellate jurisdiction where the Constitution has declared their jurisdiction shall be original, and original jurisdiction where the Constitution has declared it shall be appellate, the distribution of jurisdiction made in the Constitution is form without substance." Thus it follows that any act of Congress which attempts to change the constitutional definition of impeachable high crimes and misdemeanors, by adding to the list some offense unknown to the parliamentary law of England as it existed in 1787, is simply void and of no effect.

2010. Argument that judges may be impeached only for judicial misconduct occurring in the actual administration of justice in connection with the court.

That the framers of our Constitution well knew the limitations they were imposing upon the right of impeachment is further attested by the fact that in the original draft of that great document the language was "for treason, bribery, or maladministration," and the word "maladministration" has crept into some of the constitutions of our several States. Upon the consideration of that question on the floor of the convention it was moved to strike out "maladministration" and insert "other high crimes and misdemeanors," and for the very reason that the term "maladministration" was a loose term that might mean, under the decisions of the Senate in the future, much or little; that it might cover impeachments at one period of time by one party in power that it would not cover at another period of time with another party in power. They struck it out because it was too large a term, too loose a term, and they inserted in its place those definite words, "high crimes and misdemeanors," taken from the English constitution with parliamentary construction already attached.

We took that provision from the English constitution and with it we took the interpretation that was placed upon it by the . . . law of Parliament, established by the adjudications in the great tribunal. That provision meant then what it meant in England at the time. Mr. President, that provision meant then what it has meant ever since. It meant then what it always must mean. From the debates in that convention it does appear that those words were adopted with that construction upon them because it was claimed that it would be unwise to permit even the Congress of the United States, by ever making something a crime that was not then a crime, to enlarge the operation of that impeachment provision of the Constitution, or to repeal some of those things which then constituted crimes and thereby prevent the impeachment of those who committed them.

Sir, that provision of the Constitution was embodied in that great instrument with a meaning that can never be changed by the Congress of the United States. It was embodied there with a meaning which will remain the same to the end of time. It furnishes the limitation with which the power of Congress can be exercised in impeachment cases.

2015. **Argument that an impeachable offense is any misbehavior that shows disqualification to hold and exercise the office, whether moral, intellectual or physical.**

Answer to the argument that a judge may be impeached only for acts done in his official capacity. . . .

. . . The framers of the Constitution intended that the House of Representatives should have the right to impeach and the Senate the power to try a judicial officer for any misbehavior that showed disqualification to hold and exercise the office, whether moral, intellectual, or physical. . . .

The convention that framed the Constitution did not define words, but used them in the sense in which they were understood at that time.

The convention did not invent the remedy by impeachment, but adopted a well-known and frequently used method of getting rid of objectionable public officers, modifying it to suit the conditions of a new country.

In England all the King's subjects were liable to impeachment for any offense against the sovereign or the law. Floyd was impeached for speaking lightly of the Elector Palatine and sentenced to ride on horseback for two successive days through certain public streets with his face to the horse's tail, with the tail in his hands; to stand each day two hours in pillory; to be pelted by the mob, then to be branded with the letter "K" and be imprisoned for life in the Tower. The character and extent of the punishment was in the discretion of the House of Lords.

The Constitution modified the remedy by confining it to the President, Vice-President, and all civil officers, and the punishment to removal from office and disqualification to hold office in future.

That it was not intended as a punishment of crime clearly appears when we read that a party convicted shall nevertheless be liable and subject to indictment, trial, judgment, and punishment according to law.

Said Mr. Bayard, in Blount's trial:

"Impeachment is a proceeding of a purely political nature. It is not so much designed to punish the offender as to secure the State. It touches neither his person nor his property, but simply divests him of his political capacity." (Wharton's State Trials, 263.)

Subject to these modifications and adopting the recognized rule, the Constitution should be construed so as to be equal to every occasion which might call for its exercise and adequate to accomplish the purposes of its framers. Impeachment remains here as it was recognized in England at and prior to the adoption of the Constitution.

These limitations were imposed in view of the abuses of the power of impeachment in English history.

These abuses were not guarded against in our Constitution by limiting, defining, or reducing impeachable crimes, since the same necessity existed here as in England for the remedy of impeachment, but by other safeguards thrown around it in that instrument. It will be observed that the sole power of impeachment is conferred on the House and the sole power of trial on the Senate by Article I, sections 2 and 3. These are the only jurisdictional clauses, and they do not limit impeachment to crimes and misdemeanors. Nor is it elsewhere so limited. Section 4 of Article II makes it imperative when the President, Vice-President, and all civil officers are convicted of treason, bribery, or other high crimes and misdemeanors that they shall be removed from office. There may be cases appropriate for the exercise of the power of impeachment where no crime or misdemeanor has been committed.

Whatever crimes and misdemeanors were the subjects of impeachment in England prior to the adoption of our Constitution, and as understood by its framers, are, therefore, subjects of impeachment before the Senate of the United States, subject only to the limitations of the Constitution.

"The framers of our Constitution, looking to the impeachment trials in England, and to the writers on parliamentary and common law, and to the constitutions and usages of our own States, saw that no act of Parliament or of any State legislature ever undertook to define an impeachable crime. They saw that the whole system of crimes, as defined in acts of Parliament and as recognized at common law, was prescribed for and adapted to the ordinary courts." (2 Hale, Pl. Crown, ch. 20, p. 150; 6 Howell State Trials, 313, note.)

They saw that the high court of impeachment took jurisdiction of cases where no indictable crime had been committed, in many instances, and there was then, as there yet are, two parellel modes of reaching some, but not all offenders — one by impeachment, the other by indictment.

With these landmarks to guide them, our fathers adopted a Constitution under which official malfeasance and nonfeasance, and, in some cases, misfeasance, may be the subject of impeachment, although not made criminal by act of Congress, or so recognized by the common law of England, or of any State of the Union. They adopted impeachment as a means of removing men from office whose misconduct imperils the public safety and renders them unfit to occupy official position. . . .

"In examining the parliamentary history of impeachments it will be found that many offenses not easily definable by law, and many of a purely political character, have been deemed high crimes and misdemeanors worthy of this extraordinary remedy. Thus lord chancellors, and judges, and other magistrates have not only been impeached for bribery and acting grossly contrary to the duties of their offices, but for misleading their sovereign by unconstitutional opinions, and for attempts to subvert the fundamental laws and introduce arbitrary power. So where a lord chancellor has been thought to have put the great seal to an ignominious treaty, a lord admiral to have neglected the safeguard of the sea, an ambassador to have betrayed his trust, a privy councilor to have propounded or supported pernicious and dishonorable measures, or a confidential adviser of his sovereign to have obtained exorbitant grants or incompatible employments — these have been all deemed impeachable offenses. Some of these offenses, indeed, for which persons were impeached in the early ages of British jurisprudence would now seem harsh and severe; but perhaps they were rendered necessary by existing corruptions, and the importance of suppressing a spirit of favoritism and court intrigue.

"Thus persons have been impeached for giving bad counsel to the King, advising a prejudicial peace, enticing the King to act against the advice of Parliament, purchasing offices, giving medicine to the King without advice of physicians, preventing other persons from giving counsel to the King except in their presence, and procuring exorbitant personal grants from the King. But others, again, were founded in the most salutary public justice, such as impeachments for malversations and neglects in office, for encouraging pirates, for official oppression, extortions, and deceits, and especially for putting good magistrates out of office and advancing bad. One can not but be struck, in this light enumeration, with the utter unfitness of the common tribunals of justice to take cognizance of such offenses, and with the entire propriety of confiding the jurisdiction over them to a tribunal capable of understanding and reforming and scrutinizing the policy of the state, and of sufficient dignity to maintain the independence and reputation of worthy public officers." . . .

In the United States. — The Constitution of the United States provides that the President, Vice-President, and all civil officers of the United States shall be removed from office on impeachment for, and conviction of, treason, bribery, or other high crimes and misdemeanors. If impeachment in England be regarded merely as a mode of trial for the punishment of common-law or statutory crimes, and if the Constitution has adopted it only as a mode of procedure, leaving the crimes to which it is to be applied to be settled by the general rules of criminal law, then, as it is well settled that in regard to the National Government there are no common-law crimes, it would seem necessarily to follow that impeachment can be instituted only for crimes specifically named in the Constitution or for offenses declared to be crimes by Federal statute. This view has been maintained by very eminent authority. But the cases of impeachment that have been brought under the Constitution would seem to give to the remedy a much wider scope than the above rule would indicate. . . .

The purpose of impeachment, in modern times, is the prosecution and punishment of high crimes and misdemeanors, chiefly of an official or political character, which are either beyond the reach of the law, or which no other authority in the State but the supreme legislative power is competent to prosecute, and, by the law of Parliament, all persons, whether peers or commoners, may be impeached for any crimes or offenses whatever. . . .

What is an impeachable offense? This is a preliminary question which demands attention. It must be decided before the court can rightly understand what it is they have to try. The Constitution of the United States declares the tenure of the judicial office to be 'during good behavior.' Official misbehavior, therefore, in a judge is a forfeiture of his office. But when we say this we have advanced only a small distance. Another question meets us. What is misbehavior in office? In answer to this question and without pretending to furnish a definition, I freely admit we are bound to prove that the respondent has violated the Constitution or some known law of the land. This, I think, was the principle fairly to be deduced from all the arguments on the trial of Judge Chase, and from the votes of the Senate in the articles of impeachment against him, in opposition to the principle for which his counsel in the first instance strenuously contended, that in order to render an offense impeachable it must be indictable. But this violation of law may consist in the abuse as well as in the usurpation of authority.

The abuse of a power which has been given may be as criminal as the usurpation of a power which has not been granted. Can there be any doubt of this? Suppose a man to be indicted for an assault and battery. He is tried and found guilty, and the judge, without any circumstances of peculiar aggravation having been shown, fines him a thousand dollars and commits him to prison for one year. Now, although the judge may possess the power to fine and imprison for this offense, at his discretion, would not this punishment be such an abuse of judicial discretion and afford such evidence of the tyrannical and arbitrary exercises of power as would justify the House of Representatives in voting an impeachment? . . . A gross abuse of granted power and an usurpation of power not granted are offenses equally worthy of and liable to impeachment. . . .

We may therefore conclude that the House has the right to impeach and the Senate the power to try a judicial officer for any misbehavior or misconduct which evidences his unfitness for the bench, without reference to its indictable quality. All history, all precedent, and all text writers agree upon this proposition. The direful consequences attendant upon any other theory are manifest. . . .

2019. Abandonment of the theory that impeachment may be only for indictable offenses.

When sitting as a high court of impeachment the Senate is the sole and final judge of the meaning of the phrase "high crimes and misdemeanors." It has been well said that " 'Treason, bribery, and other high crimes and misdemeanors' are of course impeachable. Treason and bribery are specifically named. But 'other high crimes and misdemeanors' are just as fully comprehended as though each was specified. The Senate is made the sole judge of what they are. There is no revising court. The Senate determines in the light of parliamentary law. Congress can not define or limit by law that which the Constitution defines in two cases by enumeration and in others by classification, and of which the Senate is sole judge." And yet the Senate sitting as a court of impeachment has in no cases tried before it ever attempted to define the momentous phrase in question, and probably never will. When a new case arises nothing can be learned except what may be gleaned from the individual utterances of Senators, and from the arguments of counsel made in preceding cases, too often under the temptation to bend the precedents to the necessities of the particular occasion. One good result has, however, been the outcome of such discussion, and that is the elimination of two propositions which have perished through their own inherent weakness. On the one hand, a grotesque attempt has been made to narrow unreasonably the jurisdiction of the Senate sitting as a court of impeachment by the claim that the power of impeachment is limited to offenses positively defined by the statutes of the United States as impeachable crimes and misdemeanors.

Apart from its other infirmities, this contention loses sight of the fact that Congress has no power whatever to define a high crime and misdemeanor. On the other hand, an equally untenable attempt has been made to widen unreasonably the jurisdiction of the Senate sitting as a court of impeachment by the claim that, under the general principles of right, it can declare that an impeachable high crime or misdemeanor is one in its nature or consequence subversive of some fundamental or essential principle of government or highly prejudicial to the public interest, and this may consist of a violation of the Constitution, of law, of an official oath, or of duty, by an act committed or omitted, or, without violating a positive law, by the abuse of discretionary powers for improper motives or for an improper purpose. This expansive and nebulous definition embodies an attempt to clothe the Senate sitting as a court with such a jurisdiction as it would have possessed had the Federal Convention seen fit to extend impeachment "to malpractice and neglect of duty," or to "maladministration," a proposition rejected with a single dissent because, as Madison expressed it, "So vague a term will be equivalent to a tenure during the pleasure of the Senate."

Even that school which gives the widest possible interpretation to the Federal Constitution will hardly be willing to go so far, even under the general-welfare clause, as to write into the Constitution phrases and meanings which the framers expressly rejected, in order to accomplish what may be considered by some a convenient end. Certainly that school which still respects the canons of strict construction can not listen to such an argument. Between the two extremes, those who have made a careful study of the subject find no difficulty in reaching the obvious conclusion that the term "high crimes and misdemeanors" embraces simply those offenses impeachable under the parliamentary law of England in 1787, subject to such modifications as that law suffered in the process of reproduction. When the objection is made that the phrase thus construed covers too narrow an area, the answer is that it was the expressly declared purpose of the framers so to restrict it within narrow limits perfectly understood at the time. . . .

2020. Argument that impeachment is not restricted to offenses indictable under Federal law. . . .

Although it would seem that the question must now be considered settled, nevertheless in nearly every impeachment trial the question is raised as to the character of and offenses for which impeachment will lie. In times past men of great learning and authority have contended that no officer can be impeached except for indictable offenses, and that as there are no common-law offenses against the United States, it follows that there can be no impeachment except for an offense expressly declared and made indictable by act of Congress. This view of the matter fades away in the bright light of reason and precedent.

Such a construction would render the constitutional provision practically a nullity. Congress has defined and made indictable by statute comparatively few offenses. It would be impossible in any statute to define or describe all the various ways in which a judge or other civil officer might so notably and conspicuously misbehave himself as to justify and require his removal. Even murder is not defined in any act of Congress. When it so appears, reference to some other source must be had to ascertain the meaning of the term. Murder is not made indictable by any act of Congress, nor has any Federal court jurisdiction of that crime unless committed upon the high seas. . . .

We may therefore look to the law of England for the meaning of the term "impeachment" and of the phrase "high crimes and misdemeanors," as used in connection therewith — not so much to the statute law, nor to the common law, as generally understood, but to the common parliamentary law of England, as found in the precedents and reports of impeachment cases.

The Senate has always been governed in impeachment cases by the *lex et consuetudo parliamenti*. It requires but a brief investigation to show that according to the English parliamentary practice in vogue at and prior to the adoption of the Constitution, the greatest possible variety of offenses, not indictable, were nevertheless held proper causes for impeachment. . . .

Such is the undoubted parliamentary law of England, from which our process and practice of impeachment and the very term itself are derived. That it has been adopted and followed here is equally certain.

Judge Curtis, in his History of the Constitution (pp.260-261), says:

"The purposes of an impeachment lie wholly beyond the penalties of the statute or the customary law. The object of the proceeding is to ascertain whether cause exists for removing a public officer from office. * * * Such a cause may be found in the fact that either in the discharge of his office or aside from its functions he has violated a law or committed what is technically denominated a crime, but a cause for removal from office may exist where no offense against positive law is committed, as where the individual has from immorality, imbecility, or maladministration become unfit to exercise the office."

And Judge Story says, in section 799 of his work on the Constitution:

"Congress has unhesitatingly adopted the conclusion that no previous statute is necessary to authorize an impeachment for any official misconduct. * * * In the few cases of impeachment which have hitherto been tried no one of the charges has rested upon any statutable misdemeanor." (1 Story on Con., sec. 799.)

Such writers as Cooley and Wharton and Rawle maintain the same position and support it not only by reason, but by authority and precedent. . . .

CANNON'S PRECEDENTS

The second major legal authority on impeachment is *Cannon's Precedents of the House of Representatives*, published in 1935. Clarence Cannon served as House Parliamentarian from 1915 to 1921 before being elected as Representative from Missouri for four decades. He also served notably as Parliamentarian for many Democratic national conventions. The full text of this portion of *Cannon's Precedents* is re-printed in *Impeachment — Selected Materials*, 88-123.

454. Discussion by English and American authorities of the general nature of impeachment.

The fundamental law of impeachment was stated by Richard Wooddeson, an eminent English authority, in his Law Lectures delivered at Oxford in 1777, as follows (pp. 499 and 501, 1842 ed.):

"It is certain that magistrates and officers intrusted with the administration of public affairs may abuse their delegated powers to the extensive detriment of the community and at the same time in a manner not properly cognizable before the ordinary tribunals. The influence of such delinquents and the nature of such offenses may not unsuitably engage the authority of the highest court and the wisdom of the sagest assembly. The Commons, therefore, as the grand inquest of the nation, became suitors for penal justice, and they can not consistently, either with their own dignity or with safety to the accused, sue elsewhere but to those who share with them in the legislature.

"On this policy is founded the origin of impeachments, which began soon after the constitution assumed its present form. . . ."

Referring to the function of impeachments, Rawle, in his work on the Constitution (p. 211), says:

"The delegation of important trusts affecting the higher interests of society is always from various causes liable to abuse. The fondness frequently felt for the inordinate extension of power, the influence of party and of prejudice, the seductions of foreign states, or the baser appetite for illegitimate emoluments are sometimes productions of what are not unaptly termed 'political offenses' (Federalist, No. 65), which it would be difficult to take cognizance of in the ordinary course of judicial proceeding." . . .

455. Discussion as to what are impeachable offenses.

Argument as to whether impeachment is restricted to offenses which are indictable, or at least of a criminal nature.

In the Senate sitting for the impeachment trial of Judge Robert W. Archbald. . . .

In their brief, counsel for the respondent lay down, as the first proposition, that no offense is impeachable unless it is indictable; and, as a second proposition, and the only other proposition that they submit, is that, if the offense in order to be impeachable need not be indictable, it must at least be of a criminal nature.

As to the first proposition, the contention of counsel for the respondent is not sustained either by the language of the Constitution, by the decisions of the Senate in former impeachment cases, by the decisions of other tribunals in this country which have tried impeachment cases, or by the decisions of the English Parliament; nor is that contention sustained, so far as I have been able to read the authorities and the law writers on constitutional law, by a single American writer. . . .

I ask the Senate to consider that nowhere in that language [in the Constitution] is there any limitation as to the nature or extent of the crimes, misdeameanors, and misbehaviors in office. The Constitution does not undertake to define those terms with reference to the jurisdiction of the Senate in removing public officers for the violation of those provisions of that instrument, nor does it limit the time as to the commission of these offenses. It does not provide that the offenses shall be committed during the service from which it is sought to remove him, nor does it limit

Congress as to when it may proceed to impeach and try an offending servant. . . .

If the Constitution puts no limitation on the House of Representatives or the Senate as to what constitutes these crimes, misdemeanors, and misbehaviors, where shall we go to find the limitations? There is no law, statutory nor common law, which puts limitations on or makes definitions for the crimes, misdemeanors, and misbehaviors which subject to impeachment and conviction.

It will not be maintained either by the managers or by the counsel for the respondent that precedents bind, and yet we may well consider them, because they are so uniform on the question as to what constitutes impeachable offenses. The decisions of the Senate of the United States, of the various State tribunals which have jurisdiction over impeachment cases, and of the Parliament of England all agree that an offense, in order to be impeachable, need not be indictable either at common law or under any statute.

I desire to read briefly from some of the law writers of this country, giving their conclusions as to what constitute impeachable offenses, after they had reviewed and considered cases that have been tried in the Senate and in other forums where impeachment cases have been tried. . . .

. . . Outside of the language of the Constitution . . . there is no law which binds the Senate . . . except that law which is prescribed by their own conscience, and on that, and on that alone, must depend the result of this trial. Each Senator must fix his own standard; and the result of this trial depends upon whether or not these offenses . . . come within the law laid down by the conscience of each Senator for himself. . . .

456. Argument that a civil officer of the United States may be impeached for an unindictable offense.

By usage of the English Parliament so far back that the memory of man runneth not to the contrary, offenses were impeachable which were not indictable or punishable as crimes at common law. Therefore, the phrase "high crimes and misdemeanors" must be as broad and extended as the offense against which the process of impeachment affords protection. Every case of impeachment must stand alone, and while certain general principles control the judgment and conscience, the Senate alone must determine the issue.

. . . The conclusion is irresistible that an impeachment proceeding by a committee of the House is only an inquiry into the charges like a grand jury investigation, and an official can be impeached for high crimes and misdemeanors which are not indictable offenses. If there ever was any doubt of this, that question has been entirely set at rest in the impeachment proceedings in 1912 against Robert W. Archbald, United States circuit judge. None of the articles exhibited against Judge Archbald, on which he was impeached, charged an indictable offense, or even a violation of positive law.

457. Summary of deductions drawn from judgments of the Senate in impeachment trials.

The Archbald case removed from the domain of controversy the proposition that judges are only impeachable for the commission of crimes or misdemeanors against the laws of general application.

On January 13, 1914, on motion of Mr. Elihu Root, of New York, a monograph by Wrisley Brown, of counsel on behalf of the managers in the impeachment trial of Judge Robert W. Archbald, was printed as a public document. The following is an excerpt:

The impeachments that have failed of conviction are of little value as precedents because of their close intermixture of fact and law, which makes it practically impossible to determine whether the evidence was considered insufficient to support the allegation of the articles, or whether the acts alleged were adjudged insufficient in law to constitute impeachable offenses. The action of the House of Representatives in adopting articles of impeachment in these cases has little legal significance, and the deductions which have been drawn from them are too conjectural to carry much persuasive force. Neither of the successful impeachments prior to the case of Judge Archbald was defended, and they are not entitled to great weight as authorities. In the case of Judge Pickering, the first three articles charged violations of statutory law, although such violations were not indictable. Article four charged open and notorious drunkenness and public blasphemy, which would probably have been punishable as misdemeanors at common law. In the case of Judge Humphreys, articles three and four charged treason against the United States. The offense charged in articles one and two probably amounted to treason, inasmuch as the ordinance of secession of South Carolina had been passed prior to the alleged secessionary speeches of the respondent, and the offenses charged in articles five to seven, inclusive, savored strongly of treason. But, it will be observed, none of the articles exhibited against Judge Archbald charged an indictable offense, or even a violation of positive law. Indeed, most of the specific acts proved in evidence were not intrinsically wrong, and would have been blameless if committed by a private citizen. The case rested on the alleged attempt of the respondent to commercialize his potentiality as a judge, but the facts would not have been sufficient to support a prosecution for bribery. Therefore, the judgment of the Senate in this case has forever removed from the domain of controversy the proposition that the judges are only impeachable for the commission of crimes or misdemeanors against the laws of general application. The case is constructive, and it will go down in the annals of the Congress as a great landmark of the law.

459. On January 9, 1913, in the Senate sitting for the Archbald impeachment trial, Mr. Manager George W. Norris, of Nebraska, said in concluding argument:

The authorities are practically unanimous that a public official can be impeached for official misconduct occurring while he held a prior office if the duties of that office and the one he holds at the time of the impeachment are practically the same, or are of the same nature. The Senate must bear in mind, as stated by all of the authorities, that the principal object of impeachment proceedings is to get rid of an unworthy public official. In the State of New York it was held in the Barnard case that the respondent could be impeached and removed from office during his second term for acts committed during his first term. And in the State of Wisconsin the court held the same way in the impeachment of Judge Hubbell. To the same effect was the decision in Nebraska upon the impeachment trial of Governor Butler. . . .

460. Argument that an impeachable offense is any misbehavior or maladministration which has demonstrated unfitness to continue in office. . . .

The learned counsel for the respondent, by insisting that only indictable offenses are impeachable, would seem to be placing himself in the position of holding that the object of impeachment was punishment to the individual. This conception of the object of impeachment is entirely erroneous, and whatever injury may result to the individual is purely incidental and not one of the objects of impeachment in any sense. An impeachment proceeding is the exercise of a power which the people delegated to their representatives to protect them from injury at the hands of their own servants and to purify the public service. The sole object of impeachment is to relieve the people in the future, either from the improper discharge of official functions or from the discharge of official functions by an improper person. This view of impeachment is clearly demonstrated by the judgment which the Constitution authorizes in case of conviction and which shall extend no further than removal from office and disqualification to hold or enjoy any office of honor, trust, or profit under the Government of the United States, leaving the punishment of the individual for any crime he may have committed to the criminal court. . . .

463. On January 9, 1914, in the Senate, sitting for the Archbald impeachment trial, Mr. Manager John W. Davis, of West Virginia, said in final argument:

The issue narrows itself down to the meaning of the phrase "high crimes and misdemeanors" occurring in Article II, section 4, of the Constitution; and the respondent now renews the oft-repeated contention that this language can be used only with reference to offenses which, either by common law or by some express statute, are indictable as crimes. Every canon of construction which can be applied to this clause of the Constitution negatives the position which counsel for the respondent assume. Test it by the context, by contemporary interpretation, by precedent, by the weight of authority, and by that reason which is the life of every law, and the answer is always the same. . . .

Stated in its simplest terms, the proposition of counsel is to change the language of the Constitution so that instead of reading that—

"the judges both of the Supreme and inferior courts shall hold their offices during good behavior" — it will read that — "the judges both of the Supreme and inferior courts shall hold their offices so long as they are guilty of no indictable crime."

If the latter were the true meaning, is it conceivable that the careful and exact stylists by whom the Constitution was composed would have used an ambiguous term to express it?

But counsel ask: What shall be done with that clause which provides that in case of impeachment—

"the party convicted shall nevertheless be liable and subject to indictment, trial, judgment, and punishment according to law."

This, they insist, is a definition by implication, and signifies that the scope of impeachment and indictment is one and the same, although the mode of trial and the penalty to be inflicted may differ. We submit, on the contrary, that this clause instead of being a declaration that impeachment and indictment occupy the same field, is a recognition of the fact that the field which they occupy may or may not be identical; and, recognizing this fact, it declares merely that when the field of impeachment and the field of indictment overlap there shall be no conflict between them, but that the same offense may be proceeded against in either forum or in both. . . .

THE KELLEY MEMORANDUM

Congressman Gerald R. Ford's definition of impeachability delivered in the House of Representatives on April 15, 1970, was based largely upon a legal document prepared at his request by two constitutional lawyers, Bethel B. Kelley and Daniel G. Wyllie, when the House Judiciary Committee investigated impeachment charges against Supreme Court Justice William O. Douglas in 1970. The portions of the Kelley Memorandum which follow are from the sections entitled "Analysis" and "Conclusion." The full text can be found in *Legal Materials on Impeachment*, House Committee Print, Committee on the Judiciary, House of Representatives, 91st Congress, 2nd Session, August 11, 1970 (Washington, D.C., 1970).

A review of the past impeachment proceedings has clearly established little constitutional basis to the argument that an impeachable offense must be indictable as well. If this were to be the case, the Constitution would then merely provide an additional or alternate method of punishment, in specific instances, to the traditional criminal law violator. If the framers had meant to remove from office only those officials who violated the criminal law, a much simpler method than impeachment could have been devised. Since impeachment is such a complex and cumbersome procedure, it must have been directed at conduct which would be outside the purview of the criminal law. Moreover, the traditionally accepted purpose of impeachment would seem to work against such a construction. By restricting the punishment for impeachment to removal and disqualification from office, impeachment seems to be a protective, rather than a punitive, device. It is meant to protect the public from conduct by high officials that undermines public confidence. Since that is the case, the nature of impeachment must be broader than this argument would make it. Such conduct on the part of a judge, while not criminal, would be detrimental to the public welfare. Therefore it seems clear that impeachment will lie for conduct not indictable nor even criminal in nature. It will be remembered that Judge Archbald was removed from office for conduct which, in at least one commentator's view, would have been blameless if done by a private citizen. . . .

A sound approach to the Constitutional provisions relating to the impeachment power appears to be that which was made during the impeachment of Judge Archbald. Article I, Sections 2 and 3 give Congress jurisdiction to try impeachments. Article II, Section 4, is a mandatory provision which requires removal of officials convicted of "treason, bribery or other high crimes and misdemeanors." The latter phrase is meant to include conduct, which, while not indictable by the criminal law, has at least the characteristics of a crime. However, this provision is not conclusively restrictive. Congress may look elsewhere in the Constitution to determine if an impeachable offense has occurred. In the case of judges, such additional grounds of impeachment may be found in Article III, Section 1, where the judicial tenure is fixed at "good behaviour." Since good behaviour is the limit of the judicial tenure, some method of removal must be available where a judge breaches that condition of his office. That method is impeachment. Even though this construction has been criticized . . . as being logically fallacious, . . . it seems to be the construction adopted by the Senate in the Archbald and Ritter cases. Even Simpson, who criticized the approach, reaches the same result because he argues that "misdemeanor" must, by definition, include misbehaviour in office. . . .

In conclusion, the history of the constitutional provisions relating to the impeachment of Federal judges demonstrates that only the Congress has the power and duty to remove from office any judge whose proven conduct, either in the administration of justice or in his personal behavior, casts doubt on his personal integrity and thereby on the integrity of the entire judiciary. . . . Thus, it can fairly be said that it is the conscience of Congress — acting in accordance with the constitutional limitations — which determines whether conduct of a judge constitutes misbehavior requiring impeachment and removal from office. If a judge's misbehavior is so grave as to cast substantial doubt upon his integrity, he must be removed from office regardless of all other considerations. If a judge has not abused his trust, Congress has the duty to reaffirm public trust and confidence in his actions.

THE RIFKIND MEMORANDUM

In contrast with the broad interpretation of impeachability in the Kelley Memorandum, the Rifkind Memorandum argues for a much narrower and limited definition.
Simon H. Rifkind, counsel for Justice William O. Douglas,
presented these views in his "Memorandum on Impeachment of Federal Judges" filed with the special subcommittee of the House Judiciary Committee investigating impeachment charges against Justice Douglas in 1970. The
selection which follows is the brief "Conclusion" of the
Rifkind Memorandum. The full text can be found in *Legal
Materials on Impeachment*, House Committee Print, Committee on the Judiciary, House of Representatives, 91st
Congress, 2nd Session, August 11, 1970 (Washington, D.C.,
1970).

The constitutional language, in plain terms, confines
impeachment to "Treason, Bribery, or other high Crimes
and Misdemeanors." The history of those provisions rein-
forces their plain meaning. Even when the Jeffersonians
sought to purge the federal bench of all Federalist judges,
they felt compelled to at least assert that their political
victims were guilty of "high Crimes and Misdemeanors."
The unsuccessful attempt to remove Justice Chase firmly
established the proposition that impeachment is for *criminal* offenses only, and is not a "general inquest" into the
behavior of judges. There has developed the consistent
practice, rigorously followed in every case in this century,
of impeaching federal judges only when *criminal* offenses
have been charged. Indeed, the House has *never* impeached
a judge except with respect to a "high Crime" or "Misdemeanor." Characteristically, the basis for impeachment has
been the soliciting of bribes, selling of votes, manipulation
of receivers' fees, misappropriation of properties in receivership, and willful income tax evasion.

As Hamilton noted in the *Federalist Papers*, this strin-
gent standard for impeachment makes the unwieldy procedure unavailable to deal with such problems as disabled
judges. But that, according to Hamilton, and Story as well,
was the price the Founding Fathers deliberately paid to
insure the independence of the federal judiciary. If federal
judges commit grave crimes, they may be impeached. If
not, they are not subject to impeachment. In consequence,
while the federal judiciary has over the years suffered a few
judges who were unable to perform their duties, since 1805

it has been free from political purges and from harassment directed at the beliefs, speeches and writing of individual judges. In consequence, it has not been necessary to test Luther Martin's argument in the Chase case that the *ex post facto* clause of the Constitution forbids legislative punishment for conduct not defined in advance as punishable, or to measure impeachment for a judge's beliefs, speeches and writings against the flat prohibition contained in the First Amendment that Congress shall not abridge freedom of speech. History has, therefore, demonstrated the wisdom of the choice made by the Founding Fathers.

CONGRESSMAN DRINAN ON IMPEACHMENT

The following selection is from remarks made in the House of Representatives by Congressman Robert F. Drinan of Massachusetts on July 31, 1973, when he introduced a resolution to impeach President Nixon. His arguments focus exclusively on the impeachability of a President. Congressman Drinan is a former dean of the Boston College law school. From *Congressional Record*, 93rd Congress, 1st Session, July 31, 1973, H7049-H7051.

WHAT ACTIVITIES OR OMISSIONS AMOUNT TO IMPEACH-
ABLE CONDUCT?

All of the literature concerning the Constitutional Convention demonstrates that there is no evidence that any member of that convention expressed the opinion that impeachment was only intended to cover indictable offenses. . . .

The House of Representatives, therefore, should not wait before commencing impeachment proceedings until some clear indictable offense on the part of the President becomes manifest. The Constitution makes it clear that the Founding Fathers separated impeachment from subsequent criminal prosecution. The words "high crimes and misdemeanors" do not presuppose conduct punishable by the general criminal law. . . .

Impeachment, therefore, should not be looked upon or compared with an indictment nor should the role of the House of Representatives in considering the impeachment of a President be deemed to be that of a grand jury. Perhaps the best definition of impeachment is taken from the classic work on jurisprudence of Justice Story. This classical source states that impeachment is—

> . . . proceeding purely of a political nature. It is not so much designed to punish an offender as to secure the state against gross official misdemeanors. It touches neither his person nor his property, but simply divests him of his political capacity.

Impeachment is a noncriminal and nonpenal proceeding. Impeachment proceedings do not permit the person subject to them to claim double jeopardy if, in fact, he is tried for a crime subsequent to the impeachment.

From my review of virtually every legal and constitutional treatise ever written in American history on impeachment the term "removal from office" could be used as a synonym for "impeachment."

The framers of the Constitution were steeped in English history. They feared that the executive branch of Government might be transformed into a monarchy. At the same time the authors of the Constitution desired to perpetuate the independence of the executive branch of Government. In order to maintain a system of checks against the executive, while not really threatening the independence of that branch of Government, the framers of the Constitution provided for impeachment which, it could be argued, is a narrow exception to the separation of powers.

The history of the Constitutional Convention makes it clear that, in debating impeachment, the framers were almost totally concerned with the powers of the President. The inclusion of the "Vice President and all civil officers," now in the Constitution, was not added until shortly before the convention adjourned.

Studies of the process by which the Constitution was written make clear that the framers furnished to the House of Representatives a norm for impeachment. That norm, adopted from English law, stated that impeachment can arise from a serious failing even though such conduct or failure to act would not be under English law an indictable, common law crime. At the same time the framers of the Constitution withheld from Congress the power to inflict criminal punishment. The framers adopted the words "high crimes and misdemeanors" because they knew that these words had a limited and technical meaning.

The framers of the Constitution clearly understood the potential abuse of the power of impeachment which it conferred on the House of Representatives. They understood that impeachment could become a very partisan weapon and that its existence could threaten Presidential independence. Nonetheless they chose to give to the House of Representatives the power of impeachment as a curb on Presidential conduct which would be less than criminal but more than tolerable.

I have reluctantly come to the conclusion that a hearing on the impeachment of the President is indicated. . . .

4

The Nixon Crisis

Resolutions to impeach or to investigate the possibility of impeaching six Presidents have been introduced in the House of Representatives. These resolutions named John Tyler (1843), Andrew Johnson (1867 and 1868), Grover Cleveland (1896), Herbert Hoover (1932 and 1933), Harry S Truman (1952), and Richard M. Nixon (1972). Andrew Johnson was impeached in 1868, but the Senate fell one vote short of the required two-thirds to convict. All other attempts failed to receive approval of the House Judiciary Committee and were dropped because the charges were inadequate or ill-conceived.

Events in the late 1960's and early 1970's during the administration of President Richard M. Nixon were momentous. In the background was the war in southeast Asia which had alienated many at home and abroad. Although United States involvement in Vietnam dated back to the Truman administration and the Cold War, violent divisions among the American people emanated from large-scale military escalations begun under President Lyndon B. Johnson in the mid-1960's. Richard Nixon was elected in 1968 partly because many voters believed his pledges that he would bring our involvement there to an "honorable" end. As American troops continued fighting, even though in reducing numbers, disenchantment and discontent spread because of President Nixon's failure to respond to increasing public sentiment for withdrawal. Protests and demonstrations, some resulting in tragic violence and death as at Kent State and Jackson State Universities in 1970, added to the discord. Contributing to the malaise was increasing frustration over housing and transportation, educational and ecological problems, and a spiraling cost of living which gnawed relentlessly at family resources.

President Nixon was re-elected in November, 1972, by an overwhelming popular and electoral majority over his Democratic opponent, Senator George McGovern. The campaign was noteworthy for its rancor, vilification, and vituperation. The margin of victory was deceptive, though, as the Democratic party was badly splintered and did not support its candidate as fully as it might have. Nor did McGovern aid his cause when he committed some disastrous political blunders, including an unprecedented debacle in his choice of Vice-President. Analyses of the 1972 election indicate that many voted not so much for President Nixon as against Senator McGovern, and that what appeared to be an overwhelming "mandate of the people" may have been something altogether different.

During the months following the election hostility increased toward President Nixon. Prior to the election, diplomatic activities, military de-escalations, and administrative statements indicated that a cease-fire in southeast Asia was imminent. Suddenly, in December, 1972, heavy bombing was renewed over Hanoi. This infuriated many, even among those who had supported Nixon's Vietnam policies. The President's domestic programs encountered similar animosities. From the outset of his administration in 1969, relations with the Democratic-controlled Congress were characterized by major disagreements over spending levels and priorities, both foreign and domestic. The President sought to restrict spending by cutting back on "nonessentials," but he and Congress differed widely on both dollar amounts and programs. Congress legislated what it deemed necessary; when they differed, the President sought to limit Congressional "excesses" through executive action. His vetoes were effective because his Congressional opponents could not muster the required two-thirds majority to override. He reduced or eliminated large numbers of domestic programs and agencies, to the chagrin of many who felt the President was sacrificing minority and urban problems in favor of vested wheat, dairy, and oil interests. Especially controversial was his use of impoundment — refusing or delaying the expenditure of funds appropriated by Congress for specific programs — which created a continuing acrimonious conflict with Congress. Many, including Senators

Frank Church, Sam Ervin, and Hubert Humphrey, considered impoundment more than a political tug of war between a Republican President and a Democratic Congress. They saw instead a President bent on accumulating more and more prerogatives for himself and his office, challenging the separation of powers principle, threatening a constitutional confrontation over a doctrine of "inherent" executive powers.

By the spring of 1973 there was grave concern that President Nixon was overreaching the bounds of executive authority. On April 30, Representative John E. Moss of California urged House Democratic leaders to initiate inquiry into possible impeachment. Democratic Floor Leader Thomas P. O'Neill of Massachusetts publicly called the Moss proposal "premature" and nothing further was done. He did not elaborate on the term "premature."

During the spring and summer of 1973 a number of developments weakened President Nixon's position and led to serious consideration of impeachment. One was a shortage of meat and gasoline, accompanied by price gouging and marketing restrictions which resulted in widespread hardship and distress. Many blamed the administration, charging that agricultural and oil interests were reaping huge profits as repayment for their financial support during the President's re-election campaign. Another event which aroused the nation was the disclosure that in spite of his public statements to the contrary, President Nixon had secretly authorized heavy bombings in Cambodia lasting over several years. But even more damaging to the President's credibility was the unfolding of one of the most shocking scandals in American history, the "Watergate" affair.

In the early morning hours of June 17, 1972, District of Columbia police had arrested five men in the act of burglarizing the headquarters of the Democratic National Committee in the Watergate complex in Washington, D.C. Co-conspirators E. Howard Hunt and G. Gordon Liddy were apprehended shortly thereafter. Routine interrogation disclosed a possible link between the seven burglars and the White House. Democrats charged criminal foul play; the White House scoffed at any association with a "third-rate burglary." Democratic efforts to arouse the public and make a campaign issue of the event failed. Only after the election, when the burglars were tried and found guilty but prior to sentencing by a skeptical Federal District Judge, did defendant James W. McCord, Jr., on March 20, 1973, disclose to Judge John J. Sirica two astounding facts: (1) the burglary had been organized by persons associated with the President; and (2) after the Watergate arrests the White House had taken steps to conceal this association. The implication that the President of the United States was directly or indirectly involved in illegal interference with the election process and then with obstruction of justice shocked the nation. At the direction of Judge Sirica, routine grand jury procedures were instituted to investigate the possibility of criminal prosecutions.

Meanwhile, as a result of allegations of irregularities in collecting and expending funds in the 1972 presidential election, the Senate had established a Select Committee on Presidential Campaign Activities to look into the need for corrective legislation. Under Chairman Sam J. Ervin, Jr., of North Carolina, this committee soon began to investigate activities surrounding the Watergate break-in. Because of widespread public interest, the "Watergate Committee" hearings were broadcast and televised nationally. The result was devastating. During the summer and early fall of 1973 millions heard and watched as one incredible disclosure followed another, detailing devious activities undertaken to ensure the President's re-election. The American people were stunned by revelations of how the Committee to Re-Elect the President — "C.R.E.E.P." — had infiltrated Democratic organizations; disrupted meetings and spread discordant and outrageously false rumors; and distributed smear literature which affected the outcome of Democratic primaries, widened and intensified party dissension, and weakened Democratic opposition to President Nixon. Former White House counsel John W. Dean III led a parade of advisers close to the President who testified to shocking campaign irregularities, followed by a massive effort to hide these improprieties from the American people. Indeed, to many Americans the "cover-up" was the more serious. They were willing to accept ruefully that devious campaign practices were "dirty politics as usual." But the "cover-up" by high White House officials and the President, if true, was different; it was blatant and illegal obstruction of justice by the nation's highest officer.

Among the shocking disclosures of the Ervin Committee was the existence under the aegis of the White House of a group known as the "plumbers." Organized to seek out and eliminate "security leaks" — hence the name "plumbers" — this group was responsible, in addition to the Watergate break-in, for the unlawful entry on September 3, 1971, into the office of Daniel Ellsberg's psychiatrist, Dr. Lewis Fielding. Ellsberg and Anthony Russo, Jr., had been involved in the controversial publication of the so-called "Pentagon Papers" in 1970 in an effort to end American involvement in the Vietnam war. They were later arrested for illegally disclosing classified materials and brought to trial. In an effort to "get something" on Ellsberg, the "plumbers" had broken into the files of his psychiatrist's office in Los Angeles, but had come away empty-handed. While the trial was under way, in April, 1973, President Nixon's chief domestic adviser, John D. Ehrlichman, secretly communicated to trial judge William Matthew Byrne, Jr., that the burglary was a justifiable act of national security. He also discussed with Byrne an attractive post in the government. The judge was invited to the President's San Clemente home, where he met very briefly with President Nixon. Byrne eventually interpreted this as attempted bribery, and shortly thereafter, on May 13, 1973, indignantly dismissed the charges against Ellsberg and Russo because this "untoward government intrusion" "incurably infected the prosecution" of the case. The revelation of these developments came at the same time that other shocking disclosures were coming out of the Ervin Committee hearings. Now the Washington revelations of corruption and political machinations and conspiracies were compounded by the possibility of bribery.

One of the most astounding and decisive turns in the Watergate hearings was the disclosure on July 16, 1973, by former White House aide Alexander P. Butterfield of a secret recording system to tape conversations and telephone calls of the President. Although the taping was explained by the White House as intended to preserve the conversations of the Chief Executive "for posterity," it was clear that the contents of certain tapes could verify or disprove allegations of President Nixon's personal complicity or the complicity of his associates. Within hours the President advised the Ervin Committee that he must keep the tapes confi-

dential to preserve the principles of separation of powers
and of "presidential confidentiality." To many this seemed
a devious constitutional rubric to conceal his own guilt. The
tapes and their contents thus became one of the most
controversial issues in the Watergate investigations.

But not only for the Ervin Committee. Earlier in the
year, on May 31, at the direction of the President and in
accordance with statutory regulations of the Justice Department, Attorney General Elliot L. Richardson had established the Office of Watergate Special Prosecutor to conduct a separate and independent investigation for the President. (This was a third investigatory body, in addition to
Judge Sirica's district court grand jury and the Senate select
committee.) Archibald Cox, an eminent constitutional
lawyer, was appointed Special Prosecutor, with assurances
by the President that he would have a free hand to make a
complete and unimpeded investigation. When the existence
of the tapes was disclosed, Cox asked the White House
informally for access to them. He was turned down. On
July 23, therefore, he requested the District Court to subpoena the tapes. Judge Sirica canvassed each member of his
grand jury individually if the tapes were pertinent to their
own investigation. They responded unanimously in the
affirmative. The subpoena was issued. But on July 25 the
President informed Judge Sirica that he would not comply
with the subpoena, again citing separation of powers and
presidential confidentiality. To surrender the tapes, Mr.
Nixon declared, would be "inconsistent with the public
interest and with the constitutional position of the Presidency."

As the Watergate hearings proceeded, and as both Judge
Sirica and Special Prosecutor Cox encountered additional
frustrations from the White House, more Americans reluctantly became convinced that President Nixon had either
authorized or approved many unconscionable and illegal
activities. Many others felt that if the President had not
been directly responsible for them, at least he knew about
them and had attempted the equally amoral act of trying to
prevent the American people from learning the truth. The
resignations under fire of top presidential aides John D.
Ehrlichman and H. R. (Bob) Haldeman on April 30 had not
allayed these suspicions. Increasing numbers lost faith in
the personal and political integrity of Richard Nixon and in

his ability to lead the country. Impeachment loomed as an ominous probability.

It became a reality on July 31, 1973, when Congressman Robert F. Drinan introduced the following resolution in the House of Representatives: "Resolved, That Richard M. Nixon, President of the United States, is impeached for high crimes and misdemeanors." The resolution was referred routinely to the House Committee on the Judiciary, chaired by Congressman Peter W. Rodino, Jr., of New Jersey.

Debates over the viability of impeachment had been going on even before Drinan's resolution of July 31. Administration supporters characterized criticisms of the President as base partisanship reflecting long-standing anti-Nixon animosities and radical and liberal prejudices. The President had long experienced difficult relations with the press, and he accused many in the media, especially the *New York Times*, the Washington *Post*, and some prominent television correspondents of biased reporting that encouraged impeachment talk. Presidential spokesmen also pointed out that die-hard McGovern supporters still were attacking the President. Later, when petitions and resolutions for impeachment were introduced in the House, they pointed out that every Representative who sponsored them had also endorsed McGovern. In addition to denouncing partisan attacks, Nixon supporters insisted that the President had committed no genuinely impeachable offenses. To those who argued that Nixon's conduct of the war in southeast Asia warranted impeachment, his supporters countered that he was exercising proper and legal authority; one might legitimately disagree with the President's foreign policy, they declared, but not with his constitutional right to conduct it. President Nixon's impoundment of funds and curtailment of domestic programs, they argued, were legitimate administrative options and not cause for impeachment. Even if administrative misbehavior was conceded, Administration supporters argued — in spite of the history of impeachment — the President had committed no crime and was therefore not impeachable. After the Watergate hearings disclosed possible criminal misdeeds, they insisted that without legal proof directly incriminating the President, impeachment could not be considered seriously.

Arguments in favor of impeachment had not received

widespread acceptance prior to the Watergate disclosures. Anti-war forces had insisted for years that the war in southeast Asia, aside from its immorality, was unconstitutional, that it had not been declared by Congress, and that the President was overstepping his legal and constitutional authority. But every attempt to bring about a Congressional or judicial decision to this end was unsuccessful. The same fate befell efforts to assault the President's impoundment policies. In 1971, for instance, two public housing agencies in San Francisco sued in federal court to force the release of funds impounded by the Nixon administration. Mayor Joseph L. Alioto of San Francisco joined as a private attorney to litigate the unconstitutionality of the impoundment, and the U. S. Council of Mayors adopted resolutions endorsing the actions. But the cases collapsed when the district court held that it had no legal authority to "compel the head of the Executive Branch of government to take any action whatsoever." Although in later cases, including a water pollution case in Minnesota and a highway case in Missouri, lower courts rebuffed the impoundment practice, there was no final resolution as yet in the Supreme Court. One might question the wisdom or efficacy of the President's actions, said his defenders, but not their legality.

Watergate created a different atmosphere. What had been viewed before as partisan rancor now seemed to have more political justification. There was, for instance, growing apprehension over the increasing power of the Presidency. This executive muscle-flexing had begun long before Nixon had become President; it was a phenomenon especially of the twentieth century, accelerated by the New Deal, World War II, and the Cold War. An outgrowth of fantastic technological achievement, executive domination reflected a changing country and a changing world. But the impact of what historian Arthur M. Schlesinger, Jr., (himself one of its chief architects) described as a "run-away presidency" (*The Imperial Presidency*, New York, 1973) frightened many who learned of "plumbers," "enemy lists," "White House horrors," illicit wire-taps, and domestic intelligence, activities reminiscent of Hitlerian and Soviet totalitarianism. To some, impeachment emerged as a valid weapon not only to strip President Nixon of these devious and excessive powers, but also to deter any future President from similar designs.

The immediate problem, though, was whether Richard M. Nixon had committed impeachable offenses. On July 31, 1973, when he submitted his resolution initiating the impeachment process, Representative Drinan addressed himself to that point. Speaking on the floor of the House of Representatives, he listed four specific impeachable offenses committed by President Nixon. They are listed in the following excerpts from that speech, as printed in the *Congressional Record*, 93rd Congress, 1st Session, July 31, 1973, pp. H7049-H7051:

In view of the fact that the Members of the House of Representatives act under the Constitution as the triers of fact in any impeachment proceedings it is not appropriate to set forth circumstances surrounding recent events in a way to suggest that the only possible inference from these circumstances is a conclusion that justifies impeachment. Consequently I raise questions that in my judgment the House should seek to answer. The list of questions is by no means complete or comprehensive. . . .

The questions to which the House, in an impeachment proceeding, should address itself include the following:

First. Was there any justification for President Nixon authorizing 3,630 air strikes over Cambodia between March 1969 and May 1970? This period of 14 months of intensive bombing cost $140 million. Since the Congress knew nothing of the secret raids in Cambodia was this money obtained from the Congress under "false premises" and spent in an unconstitutional manner?

Was the President, furthermore, truthful with the American people when he stated to them on April 30, 1970, that "for 5 years neither the United States nor South Vietnam has moved against enemy sanctuaries — in Cambodia — because we did not wish to violate the territory of a neutral nation"?

Did the President, moreover, acquiesce in wrongdoing when the National Security Council, headed by Dr. Henry Kissinger, ordered the falsification of military records in order to prevent disclosure of the clandestine air war on Cambodia?

Second. Were impeachable offenses committed by the President in connection with the taping of all conversations which he made on the phone and all conversations that took place in various parts of the White House? If Mr. John Ehrlichman is accurate when he stated that he talked with Mr. L. Patrick Gray, then Director of the FBI, from a phone in the President's office it was a clear violation of

Federal law since a phone was tapped without the permission of the sender or the receiver of the message.

Once again the answers to those questions with respect to the tapes may or may not be revealed in the Senate Watergate proceedings. But the House of Representatives is nonetheless not absolved from its obligation to investigate this matter insofar as it pertains to the question of impeachment — a subject over which the House has exclusive jurisdiction under the constitution.

Third. Every court that has ruled on the question of impoundment has decided against the administration. Nonetheless the impounding goes on. It was revealed on July 26, 1973, that the Secretary of Health, Education, and Welfare had withheld $1.1 billion over the past year in moneys authorized for major Federal health programs. By what right does a Federal agency refuse to spend more than a fifth of all of the expenditures appropriated by the Congress for the health services budget? Affected by this refusal to spend were Federal mental health programs, the National Heart and Lung Institute, and the National Cancer Institute — the last having been given priority by the President himself.

Fourth. The establishment of a super-secret security force within the White House itself is, of course, unprecedented in all of American history. The assumption by the President of the statutory tasks of the FBI and the CIA raise the most serious questions concerning the impeachment of a Chief Executive who in effect established a national police force accountable only to himself.

There are many other questions that could be raised concerning the legality, the constitutionality and the propriety of action and inaction by President Nixon. . . .

It will no longer do for Members of the House of Representatives to suggest that no serious question exists. Reliable national polls indicate that some 70 percent of the American people feel that the President was involved in some way in the coverup of the Watergate scandals. Almost one-fourth of the people in the Nation have expressed the opinion that the President should be removed from office.

If the House of Representatives is to be truly the House of the people we can no longer tell almost one-fourth of America's citizens that they must expect the Senate or the courts to determine whether or not the President has committed impeachable offenses. The determination of that question is a right and duty which the House has under the Constitution and a duty which the House may not delegate to any other body in America. . . .

Finally, Members of the House of Representatives

should recognize that under the constitution a proceeding with respect to his impeachment is the only way by which a President can vindicate himself. Col. George Mason made this point when he addressed the Framers of the Constitution meeting in Philadelphia. Colonel Mason recommended that the constitution provide "for the regular punishment of the Executive when his misconduct should deserve it." But Colonel Mason went on to state that the same procedure will provide "for his honorable acquittal when he should be unjustly accused." For Members of both political parties, therefore, the impeachment process should be looked upon as the only way by which the Executive will be removed from office or by which he will secure that "honorable acquittal" to which he is entitled if he has been "unjustly accused." . . .

Reaction to Drinan's resolution was mixed, and not all the President's critics greeted it with elation. The *St. Louis Post-Dispatch*, though outspokenly critical of the President, nevertheless warned against precipitous and premature action. That newspaper was soon to be among the foremost to advocate that Nixon resign, but for the time being it suggested other alternatives to the trauma of impeachment, with that procedure reserved as a last resort. On August 5, 1973, the *Post-Dispatch* commented editorially:

Congressional reaction to Representative Robert F. Drinan's resolution of impeachment against President Nixon has been generally negative, and there appears to be no chance for it to attract support at the present time. This is just as well, we think; which is not to say introduction of the resolution was ill-advised. It was not. . . .

The fact that the resolution has been introduced should give a sort of focus to congressional thoughts, and should in addition serve notice on Mr. Nixon that impeachment for "high crimes and misdemeanors," to quote the Constitution, is not beyond all possibility.

Mr. Nixon has yet to offer a detailed defense. It is certain that he headed the most corrupt Administration in American history. But the extent of his personal involvement in the crime, misconduct and contempt for the Constitution revealed as Senate investigators dig deeper into the Watergate scandal is not known. . . .

An impeachment proceeding, should it become necessary in the end, could tear the country apart and bring about most undesirable consequences. There may be other ways to get the truth. Senator Ervin's Watergate committee is following one path; Archibald Cox, the special prosecutor, is following another. And Mr. Nixon retains the option of going before the people and answering their questions.

Any notion of impeachment would seem to be premature before the Senate committee and Mr. Cox have completed their work. And we would presume Mr. Nixon would resign if he saw that impeachment was inevitable. So it seems doubtful that the bridge will have to be crossed. But just in case, it is well to have that Drinan resolution resting in the House, like a cloud on the horizon, no bigger than a man's hand.

Among the many questions raised by the Drinan resolution was whether President Nixon was impeachable for wrongs committed by his appointees. A number of criminal indictments resulted from Watergate disclosures, including former top Presidential advisers John D. Ehrlichman and H. R. Haldeman, former White House aides G. Gordon Liddy, Egil Krogh, and David Young, and others. Even prior to the Watergate revelations and entirely separate from them, former Attorney General John N. Mitchell and former Secretary of Commerce Maurice H. Stans had been indicted by a federal grand jury for obstructing justice and interfering with a Securities and Exchange Commission investigation, a scandal of Teapot Dome proportions. None would deny that President Nixon must bear the political responsibility of these misdeeds, just as any president must answer politically to the electorate for the actions of any of his subordinates. But can these illegalities and indiscretions, for which the individual perpetrators are separately punishable by courts of law, be offenses for which a President can be impeached and removed from office? This was not an issue in President Andrew Johnson's case, nor in any of the other impeachment cases, and so there is no legal precedent. Nor were there any discussions at the Constitutional Convention in 1787 which might suggest the thinking of the Framers on this subject. But when the First Congress met in 1789, the issue arose in a debate over whether Congress or the President had the authority to remove the Chief Executive's appointees. The decision that the power should be the President's reflected in part the intent that he must be held accountable for his appointees even, as James Madison said, if it might "subject him to impeachment himself, if he suffers them to perpetrate with impunity high crimes and misdemeanors against the United States, or neglects to superintend their conduct, so as to check their excesses."

The following excerpts of this discussion in the House of Representatives in 1789 are from *Impeachment — Selected Materials*, 7-20:

On motion of Mr. BOUDINOT, the House resolved itself into a Committee of the Whole House on the state of the Union, Mr. TRUMBULL in the Chair. . . .

The committee proceeded to the discussion of the power of the President to remove an officer [appointed by the President].

Mr. SMITH said he had doubts whether the officer could be removed by the President. He apprehended he could only be removed by an impeachment before the Senate, and that, being once in office, he must remain there until convicted upon impeachment. . . .

Mr. MADISON did not concur with the gentleman in his interpretation of the Constitution. What, said he, would be the consequence of such construction? It would in effect establish every officer of the Government on the firm tenure of good behaviour; not the heads of Departments only, but all the inferior officers of those Departments, would hold their offices during good behaviour. . . .

It is very possible that an officer who may not incur the displeasure of the President, may be guilty of actions that ought to forfeit his place. The power of this House may reach him by the means of an impeachment, and he may be removed even against the will of the President; so that the declaration in the Constitution was intended as a supplemental security for the good behaviour of the public officers. It is possible the case I have stated may happen. Indeed, it may, perhaps, on some occasion, be found necessary to impeach the President himself; . . .

I think it absolutely necessary that the President should have the power of removing from office; it will make him, in a peculiar manner, responsible for their conduct, and subject him to impeachment himself, if he suffers them to perpetrate with impunity high crimes or misdemeanors against the United States, or neglects to superintend their conduct, so as to check their excesses. On the Constitutionality of the declaration I have no manner of doubt. . . .

Mr. SYLVESTER . . . was of opinion that the clause relative to the removal by impeachment was intended as a check upon the President, as already mentioned by some gentlemen, and to secure to the people, by means of their representatives, a Constitutional mode of obtaining justice against speculators and defaulters in office, who might be protected by the persons appointing them. . . .

Mr. GOODHUE ... wished to make the President as responsible as possible for the conduct of the officers who were to execute the duties of his own branch of the Government. If the removal and appointment were placed in the hands of a numerous body, the responsibility would be lessened. He admitted there was a propriety in allowing the Senate to advise the President in the choice of officers; this the Constitution had ordained for wise purposes; but there could be no real advantage arising from the concurrence of the Senate to the removal, but great disadvantages. It might beget faction and party, which would prevent the Senate from paying proper attention to the public business. Upon the whole, he concluded the community would be served by the best men when the Senate concurred with the President in the appointment; but if any oversight was committed, it could best be corrected by the superintending agent. It was the peculiar duty of the President to watch over the executive officers; but of what avail would be his inspection, unless he had a power to correct the abuses he might discover.

Mr. MADISON ... It is one of the most prominent features of the Constitution, a principle that pervades the whole system, that there should be the highest possible degree of responsibility in all the Executive officers thereof; any thing, therefore, which tends to lessen this responsibility, is contrary to its spirit and intention, ... Now, if the heads of the Executive departments are subjected to removal by the President alone, we have in him security for the good behaviour of the officer. If he does not conform to the judgment of the President in doing the executive duties of his office, he can be displaced. This makes him responsible to the great Executive power, and makes the President responsible to the public for the conduct of the person he has nominated and appointed to aid him in the administration of his department. But if the President shall join in a collusion with this officer, and continue a bad man in office, the case of impeachment will reach the culprit, and drag him forth to punishment. But if you take the other construction, and say he shall not be displaced but by and with the advice and consent of the Senate, the President is no longer answerable for the conduct of the officer; all will depend upon the Senate. You here destroy a real responsibility without obtaining even the shadow; ...

From the moment their existence became known publicly, it was apparent that the tape recordings of President Nixon's White House conversations were important evidence. This applied especially to the conversations involving White House counsel John W. Dean, who had testified to the President's direct complicity in the cover-up. For this reason both the Ervin Committee and Special Prosecutor Cox sought the tapes as evidence. Informal requests were turned down, as were subsequent formal committee subpoenae. Special Prosecutor Cox then obtained a writ from United States District Judge Sirica, but on July 25 it too was rejected by the President. (This rejection was one factor which impelled Congressman Drinan to initiate impeachment proceedings on July 31.) The brief filed by White House counsel J. Fred Buzhardt defended the President's refusal to comply as necessary to preserve the fundamental principle of separation of powers. Lest some conclude that this placed Mr. Nixon above the law, Buzhardt hastily pointed out that the President was indeed accountable, but he made it perfectly clear to whom and how: the only court to which the President was "accountable under law" was the "quasi court" of the House and the Senate in the impeachment and removal process. In effect, Buzhardt asserted, the only way to get the tapes was to impeach the President. The following is from J. Fred Buzhardt's brief as printed in the *New York Times* and the Washington *Post* on August 8, 1973:

. . . To insist on the doctrine of separation of powers is by no means to suggest that the President is above the law. This is not the case. The President is accountable under the law, but only in the manner prescribed in the Constitution. The distinction was drawn vividly by Attorney General Henry Stanbery in his argument in *Mississippi* v. *Johnson*, 4 Wall. (71 U.S.) 475, 485-486 (1867):

"It is not upon any peculiar immunity that the individual has who happens to be President; upon any idea that he cannot do wrong; upon any idea that there is any particular sanctity belonging to him as an individual, as is the case with one who has royal blood in his veins; but it is on account of the office that he holds that I say the President of the United States is above the process of any court or the jurisdiction of any court to bring him to account as President.

"There is only one court or quasi court that he can be called upon to answer to for any dereliction of duty, for doing anything that is contrary to law or failing to do anything which is according to law, and that is not this tribunal [the Supreme Court] but one that sits in another chamber of this Capitol. There he can be called and tried and punished, but not here while he is President; and after he has been dealt with in that chamber and stripped of the robes of office, and he no longer stands as the representative of the Government, then for any wrong he has done to any individual, for any murder or any crime of any sort which he has committed as President, then and not till then can he be subjected to the jurisdiction of the courts. Then it is the individual they deal with, not the representative of the people." . . .

After more than a month of legal argument and court-room maneuvering, on August 29 Judge Sirica ordered the President to surrender certain tapes so that they might be examined privately in judicial chambers to determine whether the White House claim of "executive privilege" was justified. The next day the President's lawyers, J. Fred Buzhardt and Leonard Garment, appealed Sirica's order to the United States Court of Appeals. Meanwhile, the contents of the tapes remained a secret in the White House.

In the midst of these developments centering on the President, startling events unfolded around Vice-President Spiro T. Agnew. Agnew had been Governor of Maryland prior to becoming Nixon's running-mate in 1968. As a vigorous and articulate spokesman for the President, Agnew had antagonized large segments of the communications media by his forceful allegations of anti-Administration biases. Nevertheless, as the Watergate scandals were divulged and as the prospect of impeachment and removal increased the possibility of Agnew becoming President, the same press which the Vice-President had castigated expressed relief that he appeared to have had no connections with Watergate. Then during the summer of 1973 came shocking revelations of financial kick-backs to Agnew, not only while he was Governor of Maryland but even after he had become Vice-President of the United States. Agnew at first vigorously denied the allegations, even dramatically announcing on nation-wide television that he would fight to prove his innocence. The possibility of a Presidential impeachment was traumatic enough; the prospect of impeaching the Vice-President too was shattering. Then suddenly, on October 10, Agnew resigned. After plea-bargaining with Attorney General Richardson that the Justice Department would drop all charges of bribery and extortion, Agnew pleaded *nolo contendere* ("no contest") to a reduced charge of a single income tax violation, was fined $10,000, and placed on unsupervised probation for three years. Considering the criminality of Agnew's offenses, it seems his resignation forestalled an almost certain impeachment, the first of a Vice-President in our history.

Agnew's resignation added a heavy burden to an Administration already tainted by corruption. When John C. Calhoun had resigned in 1832 — the only other Vice-President to resign from that office — it was to take a seat in the Senate and to champion the cause of South Carolina and states' rights; there was no hint of corruption then. Agnew's resignation was entirely different. Furthermore, as long as Agnew had been next in line, many had been dubious about impeaching and removing Nixon, fearing his successor might be worse. Within a few days after Agnew resigned, however, it became apparent that the choice to replace him under the provisions of the Twenty-Fifth Amendment would be Congressman Gerald R. Ford of Michigan, Republican Floor Leader in the House of Representatives. (Ford was sworn in on December 6, 1973.) Even those who had opposed Ford in the political arena for almost twenty-five years readily acknowledged that "Mr. Clean" had a record of integrity and honesty. For many who had qualms about impeaching and removing Nixon lest it bring Agnew to the White House, the prospect of Ford as successor was more palatable.

Shocked by the Agnew resignation and by continuing disclosures from the Watergate investigations, and concerned that the President might be concealing incriminating evidence on the tapes, more Americans talked of impeachment as the only way to get to the truth. Speaking at a student assembly at the University of Toledo, Senator Edmund S. Muskie of Maine reflected these concerns. After giving his reasons for endorsing impeachment, Muskie underscored how President Nixon had argued earlier, when a member of the House of Representatives from California, that the President had no authority to withhold vital information. Excerpts of Muskie's speech are printed in the *St. Louis Post-Dispatch*, October 28, 1973:

A crisis the President himself has set in motion now

requires us to determine whether the President has set himself above the law. To make that determination about the President's behavior, I believe we must now begin the hearings in the House of Representatives which are the first step toward the presentation of formal impeachment charges. . . .

The Constitution gives us but one process to enforce on a president the principle that the law is supreme. When the executive ignores the commands of the courts and abuses the trust of the people, the impeachment process offers us the surest remedy.

We are not confronted by questions of petty criminality. We are faced, instead, with charges — many of them already substantiated in convincing part — of an unparalleled conspiracy to defraud the people of their right to an honest election and of a further conspiracy to defraud the courts of their power to administer justice:

Charges that spies and saboteurs were paid to disrupt a political campaign. Charges that officially authorized burglaries were committed against a private doctor's office and a political party's headquarters. Charges that suspects and key witnesses were offered bribes to keep them silent or promises to encourage them to lie. Charges that journalists and Government officials illegally lost their privacy to official wiretappers, acting without court warrant.

Charges that independent Government agencies were pressured to abandon their impartial responsibilities in order to harass and intimidate critics of the Administration and to show favoritism to friends. Charges that the head of the FBI was ordered to destroy evidence. Charges that top officials of the CIA were ordered to violate their agency's charter against interference in internal affairs. Charges that a federal judge was offered promotion while presiding over a crucial and controversial case.

And charges that a secret police agency was established in the White House with authority to break the law in order, supposedly, to protect national security.

In the Watergate affair, the President has laid claim to uncontrolled power. Some may challenge the claim from fear that it is made to block an inquiry that might deeply embarrass the President. But, more importantly, we must challenge the power behind the claim, because such authority — uncontested — could undo the whole balance of power that has made the American experiment with democracy uniquely successful.

Centralized power, the framers knew, was ultimately irresponsible. Power over information — over the knowledge which is synonymous with power — is the ultimate authority. For, as President Nixon himself said in 1972, "When information which properly belongs to the public is systematically withheld by those in power, the people soon become ignorant of their own affairs, distrustful of those who manage them, and — eventually — incapable of determining their own destinies."

More than 25 years ago, when President Truman refused to give Congress information it sought about alleged Communist subversion in his Administration, a California Congressman named Richard Nixon said this on the floor of the House of Representatives:

"The point has been made that the President of the United States has issued an order that none of this information can be released to the Congress and that therefore the Congress has no right to question the judgment of the President in making that decision.

"I say that proposition cannot stand from a constitutional standpoint or on the basis of the merits for this very good reason; that would mean that the President could have arbitrarily issued an executive order in . . . the Teapot Dome case, or any other case denying the Congress of the United States information it needed to conduct an investigation of the executive department, and the Congress would have no right to question his decision."

The contents of the White House tapes continued to be a major issue. On October 12 the United States Court of Appeals upheld Judge Sirica's order for their surrender. But the White House still refused, again claiming separation of powers and presidential confidentiality. But on October 19 President Nixon announced a surprise "compromise." Instead of appealing to the Supreme Court as many expected (there were also rumors that Chief Justice Warren E. Burger had privately hinted to the President that the Supreme Court might decide against him), he would permit Senator John C. Stennis, Democrat from Mississippi, in whom he had complete faith, to hear the tapes and then verify a summary of their contents which the President would provide for Special Prosecutor Cox. But Cox rejected the President's proposal because it failed to comply with the subpoena and because a verified summary of the tapes would not be admissible evidence in any prosecution he might seek. The President thereupon angrily instructed Cox to cease his court action to obtain the tapes. Cox refused. On Saturday evening, October 20, in what was dubbed the

"Saturday Night Massacre," President Nixon announced the summary dismissal of Special Prosecutor Archibald Cox. The President first requested Attorney General Elliot L. Richardson, nominally Cox's superior in the Justice Department, to dismiss Cox. Richardson refused and immediately resigned, asserting that the President had reneged on his earlier assurances of independence for the Special Prosecutor. Deputy Attorney General William D. Ruckelshaus also refused to dismiss Cox and he too resigned. The President then appointed Solicitor General Robert H. Bork to be Acting Attorney General, and Bork dismissed Cox. Three days later, on October 23, the President abolished the Office of Watergate Special Prosecutor completely.

Public reaction to the "Saturday Night Massacre" went strongly against the President. Members of Congress were besieged with more than 200,000 telegrams critical of Mr. Nixon. Talk of impeachment spread on Capitol Hill as at least twenty impeachment resolutions were introduced in the House of Representatives. The circumstances of the "Saturday Night Massacre" added seriously to existing reservations about the President's integrity. Rumors abounded that Cox had "found something" and that the President was using constitutional jargon deviously to conceal his own criminal complicity. Yet none could deny that he had the legal authority to dismiss subordinates who publicly defied him. Then suddenly the Cox dismissal assumed new dimensions when that act itself was revealed as a possible criminal violation by the President. In a suit filed in the District Court in Washington, D.C., Ralph Nader (later stricken by the court as a plaintiff "for lack of standing"), Senator Frank E. Moss of Utah, and Representatives Bella S. Abzug of New York and Jerome R. Waldie of California claimed that Cox was not a Presidential appointee, that his office existed by Congressional statutory authority, and that Bork, acting for the President, had dismissed Cox illegally. The following excerpt is from the ruling of United States District Judge Gerhard A. Gesell in Civil Action No. 1954-73, filed November 14, 1973, in the United States District Court for the District of Columbia:

. . . The discharge of Mr. Cox precipitated a widespread concern, if not lack of confidence, in the administration of justice. Numerous bills are pending in the Senate and House of Representatives which attempt to insulate the Watergate inquiries and prosecutions from Executive interference, and impeachment of the President because of his alleged role in the Watergate matter — including the firing of Mr. Cox — is under active consideration. Given these unusual circumstances, the . . . effort to obtain a judicial determination as to the legality of the Cox discharge falls squarely within the recent holding of the United States Court of Appeals for the District of Columbia Circuit in *Mitchell* v. *Laird*. . . .

The duties and responsibilities of the Office of Watergate Special Prosecutor were set forth in a formal Department of Justice regulation, as authorized by statute. . . . He was to remain in office until a date mutually agreed upon between the Attorney General and himself, and it was provided that "The Special Prosecutor will not be removed from his duties except for extraordinary improprieties on his part." . . . Less than four months later, Mr. Cox was fired by defendant [Acting Attorney General] Bork. It is freely admitted that he was not discharged for an extraordinary impropriety. (See Defendant's Brief in Opposition to Plaintiffs' Motion for Preliminary Injunction, at 13.) Instead, Mr. Cox was discharged on the order of the President because he was insisting upon White House compliance with a Court Order which was no longer subject to further judicial review. . . .

The issues presented for declaratory judgment are whether Mr. Cox was lawfully discharged by defendant on October 20, while the regulation was still in existence, . . .

It should first be noted that Mr. Cox was not nominated by the President and did not serve at the President's pleasure. As an appointee of the Attorney General, Mr. Cox served subject to congressional rather than Presidential control. See *Myers* v. *United States*, 272 U.S. 52 (1926). The Attorney General derived his authority to hire Mr. Cox and to fix his term of service from various Acts of Congress. Congress therefore had the power directly to limit the circumstances under which Mr. Cox could be discharged . . . and to delegate that power to the Attorney General . . . Had no such limitation been issued, the Attorney General would have had the authority to fire Mr. Cox at any time and for any reason. However, he chose to limit his own authority in this regard by promulgating the Watergate Special Prosecutor regulation previously described. It is settled beyond dispute that under such circumstances an agency regulation has the force and effect of law, and is binding upon the body that issues it. . . .

Even more directly on point, the Supreme Court has twice held that an Executive department may not discharge one of its officers in a manner inconsistent with its own regulations concerning such discharge. . . . The firing of Archibald Cox in the absence of a finding of extraordinary impropriety was in clear violation of an existing Justice Department regulation having the force of law and was therefore illegal. . . .

The Gesell decision, though subject to appeal, immediately elicited comparisons with President Andrew Johnson's violation of the Tenure of Office Act, and many wondered if it might trigger reactions similar to those in 1868. It did not. One reason was that prior to the Gesell decision the President had re-established the Office of Watergate Special Prosecutor, and in naming Houston attorney Leon Jaworski to that position Mr. Nixon announced that the White House would cooperate fully with him. The main reason, though, was another surprising twist involving the controversial tapes. On October 23 attorneys J. Fred Buzhardt and Leonard Garment declared that the White House would comply with the subpoena issued three months earlier and surrender the tapes to Judge Sirica. The controversy seemed settled. Now the country would learn what was on the tapes.

Then came the bombshell. On October 31 Buzhardt announced that two of the tapes itemized in the subpoena had never existed, explaining that the recording machine had run out of tape and no one had re-loaded it; it was simply a mechanical oversight. But not knowing about that oversight, Buzhardt said, the White House had merely assumed the tapes existed. Adding to the incredibility of the announcement was that the two non-existing tapes would have covered crucial Presidential conversations with White House counsel John Dean and former Attorney General John Mitchell, two of the most controversial figures in the unfolding scandals. Judge Sirica immediately ordered an investigation. But there was more to come. On November 21 White House attorneys notified Judge Sirica of another disappearance: eighteen and one-half minutes of a taped conversation between the President and H. R. Haldeman had apparently been wiped out by a mysterious humming sound, and the part obliterated happened to be a discussion dealing with the Watergate break-in. Again the reaction was shock and unbelief. Sirica tried doggedly to find explanations. The President's personal secretary, Miss Rose Mary

Woods, testified that she may have accidentally erased about five minutes of the tape, but there was no explanation for the remainder. After several weeks of frustrating hearings, Judge Sirica named a panel of six experts to determine the cause of the buzzing sound. They reported back on January 15, 1974, and without flatly saying as much, they strongly suggested that the erasures were deliberate. The implications were shocking. The text of that report appeared in the *St. Louis Post-Dispatch*, January 18, 1974:

Text of a report to United States District Judge John Sirica by a panel of technical experts that analyzed an 18-minute gap in a tape recording made of a conversation June 20, 1972, between President Nixon and H. R. Haldeman, then his chief of staff.

In response to your request we have made a comprehensive technical study of the White House tape of June 20, 1972, with special attention to a section of buzzing sounds that lasts approximately 18.5 minutes. Paragraphs that follow summarize our findings and indicate the kinds of tests and evidence on which we base the findings.

Magnetic signatures that we have measured directly on the tape show that the buzzing sounds were put on the tape in the process of erasing and rerecording at least five, and perhaps as many as nine, separate and contiguous segments. Hand operation of keyboard controls on the Uher 5000 recorder was involved in starting and again in stopping the recording of each segment. The magnetic signatures observed on the tape show conclusively that the 18.5-minute section could not have been produced by any single, continuous operation. Further, whether the foot pedal was used or not, the recording controls must have been operated by hand in the making of each segment.

The erasing and recording operations that produced the buzzing section were done directly on the tape we received for study. . . . We have examined the entire tape for physical splices and have found none. Other tests that we have made thus far are consistent with the assumption that the tape is an original and not a rerecording. . . .

The buzzing sounds themselves originated in noise picked up from the electrical power line to which the recorder was connected. Measurements of the frequency spectrum of the buzz showed that it is made up of a 60 cycles per second fundamental tone, plus a large number of harmonic tones at multiples of 60. Especially strong are the third harmonic at 180 and the fifth harmonic at 300 cycles per second. . . .

Can speech sounds be detected under the buzzing? We think so. At three locations in the 18.5-minute section, we have observed a fragment of speech-like sound lasting less than one second. Each of the fragments lies exactly at a place on the tape that was missed by the erase head during the series of operations in which the several segments of erasure and buzz were put on the tape. Further, the frequency spectra of the sounds in these fragments bear a reasonable resemblance to the spectra of speech sounds.

Can the speech be recovered? We think not. We know of no technique that could recover intelligible speech from the buzz section. Even the fragments that we have observed are so heavily obscured that we cannot tell what was said.

In developing the technical evidence on which we have based the findings reported here, we have used laboratory facilities, measuring instruments, and techniques of several kind, including: Digital computers located in three different laboratories, specialized instruments for measuring frequency spectra and waveforms. . . .

In summary we have reached complete agreement on the following conclusions:

(1) The erasing and recording operations that produced the buzz section were done directly on the evidence tape.

(2) The Uher 5000 recorder designated Government exhibit number 60 probably produced the entire buzz section.

(3) The erasures and buzz recordings were done in at least five, and perhaps as many as nine, separate and continuous segments.

(4) Erasure and recording of each segment required hand operation of keyboard controls on the Uher 5000 machine.

(5) Erased portions of the tape probably contained speech originally.

(6) Recovery of the speech is not possible by any method known to us.

(7) The evidence tape, in so far as we have determined, is an original and not a copy.

Richard H. Bolt, Franklin S. Cooper, James L. Flanagan, John G. (Jay) McKnight, Thomas G. Stockham Jr., Mark R. Weiss.

Judge Sirica closed his special hearings on the tape discrepancies on January 18, 1974, with the following statement: "The court has concluded from the evidence now before it that the possibility of unlawful tampering with or suppression of evidence is sufficient to merit grand jury scrutiny."

Others had reached similar conclusions earlier. Throughout the fall and winter of 1973, as the incredible saga of the missing and erased tapes unfolded, one shocking disclosure of "White House horrors" after another emerged from the Watergate investigations. Especially after Gerald R. Ford was inaugurated Vice-President, insuring a Republican successor, the pressure mounted for President Nixon's removal, either by resignation or by impeachment. *Time* magazine, often a supporter of Nixon programs, published an editorial calling for the President to resign. Other middle-of-the-road or normally conservative-leaning publications indicated agreement. Prominent among these was *The Wall Street Journal*, an erstwhile strong supporter of Mr. Nixon, which on December 5, 1973, joined in the demand for impeachment, and in so doing produced a lengthy list of Richard Nixon's impeachable offenses (re-printed with permission of *The Wall Street Journal*, © 1973, Dow Jones & Company, Inc. All Rights Reserved):

What has Richard Nixon allegedly done to have so many people calling for his head?

Well, his various accusers have been drawing up their own unofficial Articles of Impeachment in recent weeks — a not altogether academic exercise, because their lists are the starting point for an investigation now underway by the House Judiciary Committee. Here then, is a list of the most serious charges against Mr. Nixon to date, or at least the charges on which his accusers agree. It is culled from lists compiled by Americans for Democratic Action, Ralph Nader, the American Civil Liberties Union, a team of public interest lawyers headed by William Debrovir, the AFL-CIO and 40 U.S. Representatives, who have introduced resolutions calling for Mr. Nixon's impeachment.

For convenience, the charges are grouped in five categories. Offenses against individuals, against justice and against government; offenses committed in financing Mr. Nixon's re-election campaign; and offenses committed for his personal enrichment. They are as follows:

Alleged Offenses Against Individuals

That the President ordered taps placed on the phones of 13 Government officials and four newsmen without first obtaining a court order, as required by law.

That he ordered the Internal Revenue Service to harass, by means of tax audits and investigations, leading Democrats, opponents of the Indo-china war, newsmen and other White House "enemies."

That he approved a "domestic intelligence plan" for gathering information about anti-war demonstrators, black extremists and others by unlawful means: burglary, wiretapping, bugging and opening of mail.

That he ordered creation of a special investigations unit in the White House, known as the "plumbers," which broke into the Los Angeles office of the psychiatrist of Daniel Ellsberg, then on trial for giving the Pentagon Papers to newsmen.

That he secretly recorded conversations in his office and over the phone, without the knowledge of the other participants, violating rules of the Federal Communications Commission.

That he ordered the unjustified prosecution of political dissenters in Camden, N.J., Harrisburg, Pa., Gainesville, Fla., and elsewhere, and that there was an improper use of at least 13 grand juries to investigate dissenters.

Alleged Offenses Against Government

That he caused re-election committee personnel to break into the offices of the Democratic National Committee in the Watergate office building and to place a tap on one of the committee's phones.

That he usurped the war-making powers of Congress when he ordered the bombing of neutral Cambodia and then deliberately concealed the bombing from Congress and the American people.

That he usurped Congress's power of the purse by refusing to spend some 40 billion dollars of appropriated funds.

That he interfered with a free press by the use of wiretaps on reporters' phones, FBI investigations of newsmen, threats of criminal prosecution against papers that published the Pentagon Papers, and arrests of reporters.

Alleged Offenses Against Justice:

That he tried to influence the judge in the Ellsberg trial by suggesting that he might be appointed director of the FBI.

That he withheld information from the court about the break-in at the office of Mr. Ellsberg's psychiatrist.

That he tried to cover up the involvement of White House officials and officials of his re-election committee in the Watergate affair. That the cover-up involved destroying documentary evidence, concealing the existence of evidence, promising executive clemency and paying money to the Watergate defendants, suborning perjury in their trial, trying to limit the FBI investigation, and the false use of the Central Intelligence Agency.

That he fired Special Prosecutor Archibald Cox when Mr. Cox refused to agree to Mr. Nixon's proposed "compromise" on making White House tapes available. The firing violated Justice Department regulations and assurances given to the Senate about the independence of the special prosecutor.

Alleged Campaign Financing Offenses

That he solicited and obtained illegal campaign contributions from seven corporations by promising Government benefits or threatening to withhold benefits.

That he obtained a contribution of $100,000 from International Telephone and Telegraph Corp., in return for persuading the antitrust division of the Justice Department to permit ITT to keep the Hartford Fire Insurance Co.

That he obtained a promise of a $2,000,000 campaign contribution from Associated Milk Producers Inc., a dairy co-operative, in exchange for reducing imports of dairy products.

That he obtained at least $427,500 in contributions from three milk co-ops in return for raising price supports on dairy products.

Alleged Offenses Involving Personal Enrichment

That he got the Government to spend more than $1,000,000 on his San Clemente and Key Biscayne properties for improvements not required for presidential security.

That he evaded federal income taxes by claiming $570,000 in deductions for the gift of some of his papers to the National Archives. The gift was allegedly not deductible because it was made after the cut-off date set by law.

By January, 1974, when Congress convened for the second session of the Ninety-Third Congress, the House Judiciary Committee had taken important steps in preparation for impeachment hearings. Chairman Peter W. Rodino had appointed veteran trial attorneys John M. Doar and Albert E. Jenner as majority and minority counsel. President Nixon placed equally experienced and respected James D. St. Clair in charge of the White House legal staff. They organized their staffs and began gathering evidence. On

February 5 the Judiciary Committee divided its staff into six "task forces," each concentrating on investigating a different category of allegations against the President. They were: (1) allegations concerning domestic surveillance activities conducted by or at the direction of the White House; (2) allegations concerning intelligence activities conducted by or at the direction of the White House for the purposes of the presidential election of 1972 (political spying); (3) allegations concerning the Watergate break-in and related activities, including alleged efforts by persons in the White House and others to "cover up" such activities and others; (4) alleged improprieties in connection with the personal finances of the President; (5) allegations concerning efforts by the White House to use agencies of the executive branch for political purposes, and alleged White House involvement with illegal campaign contributions; and (6) allegations concerning other misconduct that does not fall within one of the foregoing categories, such as the secret bombing of Cambodia and the impoundment of funds. The countdown to impeachment had begun.

For the American people the trauma of a presidential impeachment seemed imminent. For this reason it is important that they understand what impeachment means — that it is only the first step taken in the House of Representatives to determine whether the President has committed an offense serious enough to be tried in the Senate. It is equally important that the American people understand the offenses for which the President might be impeached. They can be either criminal or political. They must be serious offenses. They must be considered with impartiality and without personal or partisan prejudice.

Based upon the history and meaning of impeachment, Richard M. Nixon *can* be impeached. That does not mean that he is guilty and should be removed from office. It means only that there is sufficient reason to believe that he is responsible for political or criminal actions serious enough to fall within the Constitutional meaning of "treason, bribery, or other high crimes and misdemeanors." Whether he *should* be impeached depends upon how the House of Representatives, speaking for the American people, evaluates the severity and impropriety of those actions. If a majority of the House of Representatives feels there is sufficient evidence, the President will be impeached — he will be formally accused — and his case will be turned over to the Senate for trial. Like any other American citizen, the President of the United States is presumed innocent until found guilty by law. Only if he is found guilty in the Senate — and the Constitution requires a two-thirds vote — can President Nixon be removed from office.

As the American people contemplate what Alexander Hamilton termed a "national inquest into the conduct of public men," indecision and confusion abound. Impeachment is indeed a grave matter, so grave that many fear it might irreparably divide the country. This is one reason why some oppose it. On the other hand, many view impeachment not as something to be feared, but rather as an instrument to be used by Congress to make our representative system more viable. These sentiments were expressed by columnist Lawrence E. Taylor in the *St. Louis Post-Dispatch* on February 1, 1974: "If the United States cannot stand the pain of impeachment, then it should not have withstood the agony of World War II, or the great depression or the Civil War. But it did, and it came out of each stronger than before. So it should this time."

Two outstanding Americans, Thomas B. Curtis and Archibald Cox, differ in their views toward the impeachability of President Nixon, but they both agree that if the impeachment process itself is better understood and more wisely and judiciously utilized, it must inevitably result in improved government and governmental responsibility. Thomas B. Curtis was a Republican Representative from Missouri for nine terms from 1951 to 1969. A scholar in economics and constitutional law, an experienced and very knowledgeable legislator, former Congressman Curtis held a number of key posts in both Democratic and Republican administrations and is one of the most highly respected exponents of the "conservative" philosophy of American government. The following observations were written especially for this book:

The decision of the House Judiciary Committee and the Democratic leadership of the United States House of Representatives to proceed with the resolution to impeach Republican President Richard M. Nixon is the result of the constant prodding of an influential group in the news media. The charges upon which the impeachment resolution rests have been developed by this group in their public forums — television, radio, newspapers and magazines — where the rules of evidence have no application and the presentations tend to be *ex parte*. It is just now, early 1974, that the court and legislative proceedings have reached a point where matters can be reported to the public with some assurance that attention has been paid to this evidentiary discipline.

The fact that the move to impeach President Nixon derives its impetus from certain leaders of the fourth estate rather than from leaders of the opposing political party is significant, as is the fact that the first investigating action by Congress was undertaken incongruently by the Senate, the body required under the Constitution to sit as a court to determine guilt or innocence if sufficient evidence in the judgment of the House of Representatives was available to proceed with a formal trial of impeachment.

Throughout the year 1973 and even up to the present time (March, 1974) there has been a reluctance on the part of the Congressional leaders of the Democratic Party which controls both houses of the Congress to take up the charges and examine them. This reluctance can stem from four sources: (1) the Democratic leaders do not think the charges are well founded; (2) they or the immediate past Democratic Presidents are, or have been, guilty of similar offenses; (3) they are not certain that the charges, if substantiated, constitute grounds for impeachment; and (4) they may think that the election process provides better discipline than the impeachment process to keep the body politic healthy.

It is necessary to set forth and categorize the various charges levelled against President Nixon since the 1972 election to pinpoint those which might be substantiated by evidence and which might be grounds for impeachment. I do not think it is unfair to say that the news media in pushing for impeachment have done little to distinguish between charges with little or no evidence to support them and charges with substantial evidence, charges which if proved might be impeachable and those which even if proved would not be, and charges which are basically political in nature and probably should be left to the discipline of the election process and those which are not.

The charges aired in the news media are:

    A. Relating to the election process —

        (1) Interference with the election process by the illegal act of attempted burglarizing the Democratic National Committee Headquarters at the Watergate Inn.

        (2) Violation of the election laws in respect

to soliciting, receiving and reporting financial contributions.

(3) Accepting campaign donations in return for political favors.

(4) Obstructing justice in respect to the prosecution of individuals involved in the first three charges.

B.   Personal —

(1) Taking personal federal income tax deductions for donations of papers and treating sale of New York house as non-taxable.

(2) Not paying California state income tax.

(3) Using federal funds improperly to enhance the value of homes in California and Florida.

(4) Receiving for possible personal conversion a gift of $100,000 from Howard Hughes via Bebe Rebozo.

C.   Abuse of Presidential powers —

(1) Authorizing the burglary of psychiatrist office to obtain records of a patient alleged to have stolen papers vital to national security (Ellsberg case).

(2) Failing to turn over Presidential records relating to investigations by the Department of Justice, the grand jury and Congressional committees.

(3) Failure to obey court subpoenas to turn over records.

(4) Tampering with tapes of recorded conversations which might be legal evidence.

(5) Firing Special Prosecutor Archibald Cox.

(6) Using IRS to get at political enemies.

D.   Usurpation of powers —

(1) Bombing Cambodia.

(2) Impounding funds.

(3) Influencing independent government agencies improperly.

It appears that all items under B (Personal) are without sufficient substantiation. If substantiated, however, items (3) and (4) could constitute impeachable "high crimes and misdemeanors" under its most strict definition, *viz*: that there must be criminality in the acts and that serious political matters devoid of criminality are insufficient to sustain removal from office.

The items under D (Usurpation of powers) are political matters which are best suited for treatment by the election process as opposed to the impeachment process. Furthermore, Congress has ample powers to correct errors in these areas *if it cares to exercise them*.

Several important matters run through the charges under A (Relating to the election process) and C (Abuse of Presidential power). One is the responsibility for the acts of subordinates appointed by the President and the responsibility of the President to act in case of mis-feasance and possibly non-feasance on their part. Another is the power to remove unilaterally an official appointed with Senate confirmation. (This issue was decided in favor of the Presidency in the impeachment proceedings against Andrew Johnson). Finally, the issue of turning over presidential correspondence and materials is an important political matter historically and in theory. In the present instance it is unfortunately tied in with the process of investigating and prosecuting individuals for crimes. Privileged communications are not unknown in the English common law and have been respected by the federal legislature and the various state legislatures. They have long been a burden to our prosecuting officials in performing their duties: to name a few — between husband and wife, lawyer and client, doctor and patient, clergyman and communicant, and recently between a reporter and his informant. The pros and cons of executive privilege should be considered in this broad context.

Item C (1) raises a serious political issue, namely the official's actions or actions officially sanctioned in the name of national security, against enemies at home and abroad. This also covers threats to domestic tranquility in time of peace; but even more significant and more difficult to reconcile with our basic moral concepts is the type of actions sanctioned in time of war. The purloining and publishing of the Pentagon Papers and other publication of matters deemed to be security leaks certainly bear on this important political issue of guarding national security and maintaining domestic tranquility. Such matters seem better left to the election process and not be interjected into impeachment proceedings. Otherwise, it is hard to conceive anyone holding political office or even working for the Government.

Items A (1), (2), and (3) spell out areas where considerable reform in our laws have been badly needed for some time. The best way to proceed, it seems to me, is to use the Watergate exposures as the impetus to get through the reforms. There is enough blame for our election laws and campaign financing and the practices carried on under them, being in the sorry shape they are in, without politicians of either party, or concerned or unconcerned citizens, trying to pass the blame on to the other. It almost appears to be, in light of the news reporting, a question of who gets caught. And yet the bulk of our elected office holders and appointed officials, in spite of this bad situation, are totally decent and honest.

The most serious of the possible impeachment charges lie in the alleged obstruction of justice and tampering with evidence, and yet this is almost inextricably woven in with the important executive privilege of communication. President Nixon is not wrong in underscoring this important right. His critics have been gravely at fault in not discussing this issue with the importance it deserves and instead passing off all attempts of the President to discuss it as if he were simply using it as an excuse to protect himself and some of his appointees from prosecution, even if this were the case.

I think a thoughtful House of Representatives may come out quite strongly in favor of hammering down once and for all the right of the President to keep confidential communications made to him, albeit this may permit a less than scrupulous President to slow down the prosecution of law violators in some instances. The check on this abuse lies with the people every four years when they elect the President.

Most members of the Congress, whatever their party affiliation or political philosophy, have concluded that it is important that the charges levelled against the President be fully and soberly investigated and considered in order that faith in representative government be strengthened in the minds of the people. This can best be done by having the Judiciary Committee undertake the preliminary work and report its recommendations to the House of Representatives. The recommendations should not be limited, though, to "no action" or "further action to impeach the President." They should spell out specific areas where reform in our election and political processes should be made in light of the Committee's study. The Committee's report should clarify the impeachment process itself so that, if feasible, it may become a more useful tool in the representative government process, dovetailing it in with the election process. Suggestions might also be made how the news reporting process, so vital to representative government, can be improved, at the same time underscoring the essential role it plays in making the system work, with special reference to the Watergate situation. Most important, though, must be the determination that the country emerge from this experience with a strengthened faith in the workability of the American system of representative government.

Archibald Cox is one of the leading constitutional lawyers in the United States. Following the "Saturday Night Massacre," Professor Cox returned to the Harvard Law

School. On January 22, 1974, he addressed the students of Amherst College on the subject of impeachment:

Regardless of the outcome, the value of the proceeding will depend upon whether the process is so conducted that the country perceives it as a fair and legitimate measure for restoring integrity to government. If President Nixon should be impeached and convicted, the question of legitimacy will be paramount. If President Nixon is acquitted, the country will still need assurance about the integrity of that conclusion. Whatever the event, we may fairly ask that the leadership build better for the future than their predecessors at the impeachment of Andrew Johnson.

The central challenge is to formulate the principles — the general standards of conduct — by which a President is to be judged in a proceeding that vacates, without direct expression of the popular will, a choice made by the people — in this case overwhelmingly made by the people — in the regular election only a few years before. Too much discussion, both public and private, has been concerned either with loose generalities about the ultimate question of impeachment *vel non*, or with the excitement and speculation stirred by particular disclosures. Too little hard debate has focussed upon what should be impeachable offenses — upon why some wrongdoing should be grounds for impeachment while other misconduct is left to popular judgment at the polls. I am convinced that the legitimacy of the final conclusion in the view of the American people will depend upon the success of counsel and other public men in formulating general standards of conduct fairly applicable to any President, and in educating the public upon their meaning and legal and moral base. For Democratic Senators and Representatives to keep silent upon the ground that impeachment is a Republican problem and for Republicans to keep silent while they test the political winds is to deny the country the debate necessary to educated self-government and the development of governmental institutions.

A priori we might give [two] polar meanings to the "high crimes and misdemeanours" for which a President, a judge or any other civil officer may be impeached.

(1) William Giles, President Jefferson's majority leader in the Senate, advised his colleagues during the proceedings against Supreme Court Justice Samuel Chase that "impeachment is nothing more than an enquiry, by the two Houses of Congress, whether the office of any public man might not be better filled by another." Justice Chase was

acquitted. The view of impeachment expressed by Giles never again had serious support (unless one counts as "serious" the speech of Congressman Gerald Ford a few years ago advocating the impeachment of Justice Douglas).

(2) The strictest view of the constitutional phrase "high crimes and misdemeanours" holds that impeachable offenses are confined to violations of the criminal law and to "high," *i.e.* very serious crimes, whether felonies or misdemeanours. . . . The weight of the argument is against it. The English Parliamentary precedents, which were familiar to the Founding Fathers, included instances of non-criminal conduct and, although the Founding Fathers desired to cut back on the precedents, the constitutional phrasing makes it unlikely that they chose technical criminality as the line of demarcation. . . . The recorded debates at the Philadelphia Convention and the subsequent expositions of the Framers make it pretty clear that impeachment was intended to be a vehicle for dealing with officials whose wrongs require removal from office even though not technically criminal. . . .

We are left with a third view: that "high crimes and misdemeanours" covers some but surely not all "political," in the sense of governmental, offenses. Reaching this conclusion . . . is only the beginning of the challenge. What are the wrongs against the people, the body politics, for which a President may properly be impeached?

It would be easier if history provided a list of legitimate grounds for impeachment, but the only precedents are scattered pretty far afield from current issues. Working with a clean slate, perhaps we can best begin by asking what deep-seated needs any rule we formulate must satisfy.

The Gallup poll and like measures of public opinion report that a very large majority believe that President Nixon is guilty of covering up wrongdoing, but of those expressing an opinion, a majority oppose removal by impeachment. The difference, in my opinion, is attributable to a fear of impeachment not unlike the fear of regicide and the horror of the regicide once accomplished during the time of Cromwell and King Charles I. Of course, impeachment cannot be wholly illegitimate — the Constitution provides for it — but I think that the country has a deep, intuitive understanding that impeachment is extraordinary, radical surgery, legitimate only upon some equally fundamental wrong, doing such grave injury to the Nation as to make any incumbent's further continuance in office unacceptable even though his previous entitlement was based upon popular election.

Surely any wrong so fundamental as to require setting

aside the results of one election without holding another must be one that can be stated in general terms plainly applicable to any President at any time. The need is to quiet the fear that impeachment may be or become a partisan substitute for a premature election. Political opposition, emotion, dislike, distrust, and lack of public confidence (which may be temporary even when mixed with suspicion of some kind of wrongdoing) are not enough.

Equally surely, in my opinion, any general standard of political conduct the violation of which would support impeachment must have a broad and generally accepted moral base, understood by the country, so that again the same rule would apply to any President, so that we should not be resolving questions of public policy by impeachment, nor should we be making up new rules of conduct as we go along.

Of course, it is unnecessary to draw up a complete code of Presidential conduct. Mixing pragmatism with principle is one source of much of the creativity in Anglo-American law and government. We work eclectically up to a point, passing judgment upon particular sets of facts, but we also test our judgment by asking whether it rests upon reasons that we can articulate and apply to other situations having the same essential elements, with enough generality both in scope and continuity, to give guarantees against caprice, prejudice, self-interest or unreasoned emotion.

So here, the articulation of minimum acceptable standards of conduct for any President or high executive officer can begin with facts proved or assumed. It is fair to say that evidence may be available to show that President Nixon's lawyers and accountants, without deliberate misrepresentation, zealously sought every loophole and cut every corner in an effort to avoid or minimize the payment of taxes; to show that others acting on his behalf likewise stretched every possible point to add to the convenience and comfort of Key Biscayne and San Clemente at public expense; and, finally, to show that in some cases they claimed more than the law allows. Bad taste? Surely. Avaricious? Yes. Bad leadership? Again, surely. Morally shabby? I think so, even though the same shabbiness infects thousands of tax returns and expense accounts. Grounds for impeachment? I wonder. We are hardly prepared to say that any officer of the United States who, without concealing or misrepresenting material facts, claims a tax deduction not due should be removed from office. If not, does my phrasing omit some essential element in President Nixon's situation? What makes the omitted element decisive?

Let us try again. Is it tolerable or a high offense against

the liberty and security of a whole people for a President to approve in principle electronic surveillance, mail covers, and burglaries for the purpose of gathering domestic intelligence, over the objection of the established agencies, to set in motion a small force of his own irregulars — the Caulfields, Ulasewiczes, Liddys and Hunts — who will operate from the Executive Offices outside all the regularizing rules and procedures of the established agencies in order to effectuate Administration policy and political objectives, and to hamper inquiry into their activities?

Move to a third area. The President's duty is to see that the laws are faithfully executed. Is it an impeachable violation of this responsibility for him to refrain for months from any form of personal intervention when there is first suspicion and later at least some evidence that his highest personal aides and party officials are obstructing justice by covering up criminal misconduct, for him to withhold disclosure and refuse evidence when investigation leads to papers taken into his files, and for his aides, apparently with his approval, to cooperate with those seeking to avoid indictment and conviction?

I do not imply answers to these questions, nor do I suggest that my factual predicates represent the actual facts. The evidence may show more or less. The point I wish to emphasize is that it is past time for all those deeply concerned with our government to bend some of their time and effort away from the fun of factual disclosures to the very arduous task of formulating and thus creating a substantive law of impeachment where now there is none. Whether the present proceedings help to rebuild confidence in our system of government or push us further down the slope to cynicism and despair will depend upon the ability of the House Judiciary Committee to sense the as-yet-unstated moral intuition of the country and articulate it in operative principles by which President Nixon's conduct can be judged . . . .

Confidence in the institutions of government and mutual trust between the elected governors and the governed had begun to erode long before Watergate, but surely the danger of a long slide into general cynicism, distrust and despair has been intensified by the evidence giving reason to believe that power, position and the very processes of government were criminally perverted at or near the very highest level of executive office for the sake of building or perpetuating personal and political power. the first essential in reversing the trend is restoration of confidence in the integrity of government . . . .

We need to restore to government a stronger appreciation of the line separating fundamental judgments of right and wrong in the conduct of government and political life, on the one side, from mere political loyalties and political opinions on the other side. Too many of us grew up in an atmosphere of positivism and relativism in which the assertion of moral imperatives was taken as proof of ignorance and naivete, at least among those wishing to be supposed persons of experience and sophistication. Others took the imperatives for granted, supposing that the fundamentals would look out for themselves. The cynics found justification in Leo Durocher's "Nice guys finish last," or in Presidential aide Charles Colson's "It's only hard-nosed politics." One way or the other, success in gaining power took precedence and personal or party loyalty became a justification for silently going along if not actually participating in wrongdoing. It is time for a change. . . .

Watergate can be made a turning point and therefore a blessing. It has shocked out of lethargy the conscience of the Nation. Possibly my view is too self-centered and too much influenced by the moving letters I still receive, but it seems to me that the "fire storm" . . . which exploded over the week-end of October 21-22 had its source in the longing of countless simple, direct and moral people for a new measure of candor, simplicity and rectitude in the conduct of government. . . . The turn of events was extraordinary. On a Friday and Saturday the President announced that he was discharging the Special Prosecutor, terminating independent investigation of the Watergate affair and related offenses, and refusing to produce relevant tapes and documents in accordance with the order of a court. The public outcry forced an immediate 180-degree turnabout. Within days, the court was assured that the tapes and documents would be produced. Within weeks, the independence of the Watergate Special Prosecution Force was restored, the staff was retained unimpaired, and a vigorous and independent special prosecutor was appointed. This sequence of events demonstrates better than any other occurrence within memory the extent of this country's dedication to the principle that ours is a government of laws and not of men. It gave proof of the people's determination and ability to compel their highest officials to meet their obligations under the law as fully and faithfully as others. On this occasion, as so often in our history when fundamental questions were at stake, the people had a far better sense of the goals of the enterprise and needs of the nation than those claiming wider experience and greater sophistication.

The spirit is there. The power is there. The question is whether those who seek to be political leaders have the wit and will to evoke that spirit, articulate it, and take measures restoring confidence in the integrity of the government.

Congressman Thomas B. Curtis and Professor Archibald Cox, both knowledgeable and both experienced in the processes of government, have honest disagreements about what appears more and more to be the crux of the current impeachment dilemma: *What constitutes an impeachable offense?*

Despite these honest differences of opinion, and despite their mutual recognition of strong partisan overtones in American attitudes toward President Nixon, both Professor Cox and Congressman Curtis favor the *process* of impeachment.

They both see impeachment for what the Framers of the Constitution intended it to be — a procedure to insure that the person who is President of the United States does not transcend or exceed the powers that go with that high office. They recognize it as a constitutional guarantee that a President does not abuse or misuse the office of the Presidency. They see it as a means to clear the air, a method to determine guilt and to remove the guilty, but also, as George Mason said at the Constitutional Convention, a way to provide "for his honorable acquittal when he shall be unjustly accused."

Perhaps the greatest crisis facing the American people is that there are gnawing doubts about the guilt or innocence of President Nixon. The deadliest legacy of the late sixties and the early seventies, even before Watergate, was the loss of confidence by too many American people in their elected officials and in the viability of the democratic process. It has now focused on one man — President Richard M. Nixon. Rightly or wrongly, he represents to many the reasons for their mistrust in the American system. To others, rightly or wrongly, he represents what must be defended at all costs if the "American way of life" is to be preserved. Between these extremes are millions who just do not know; they are confused, uncertain, and even frightened.

But one factor does stand out. All agree that honest and decent government are absolutely essential. All agree that if the air can be cleared, the way to progress and decency in government will be open. The question is whether impeachment will open the door.

That can be answered positively only if the American people understand what impeachment is and what the Framers of the Constitution intended it to be — NOT an inquisition, NOT a purge, NOT a vendetta, but an honest and genuine and impartial "national inquest into the conduct of public men," to determine if the man or men have misused the office. The American people want and need the truth about the guilt or innocence of President Nixon. This became increasingly evident as additional indictments, bringing the total to more than twenty, were returned against former aides high in White House circles, including the two men closest to the President, John D. Ehrlichman and H. R. Haldeman, and also Charles W. Colson, special counsel to the President, and Herbert W. Kalmbach, President Nixon's personal attorney. President Nixon's staunch determination not to disclose the contents of the controversial tapes and of other documents added to misgivings about his credibility, as did his intimations that any imputations against him personally were assaults upon the office of the Presidency itself. Equally damaging were his repeated public assertions that impeachability should be limited only to criminal offenses, in spite of the history of impeachment and the intent of the Framers of the Constitution to the contrary.

Nos scimus quia lex bona est, modo quis ea utatur legitime. "We know that the law is sound so long as man uses it lawfully," said Francis Bacon. So, too, the impeachment process provided in the Constitution is sound, so long as the American people use it lawfully. Much more may be at stake than the guilt or innocence of Richard M. Nixon. At stake may well be the workability and viability of the Constitution and the American system of government. If the truth can be learned and the air can be cleared, the American people can be depended upon to act appropriately, and full faith in the Constitution and in the American system inevitably will be restored.

Appendix

Appendix A

The Constitution authorizes each house of Congress to determine its own rules of procedure. Parliamentary practice of the House of Representatives emanates from three sources: (1) rules adopted by the House; (2) *Jefferson's Manual of Parliamentary Practice*, and (3) decisions and rulings of the Speakers and of the chairmen of the Committee of the Whole. From 1797 to 1801 Vice-President Thomas Jefferson prepared the notable work that has come to be known as *Jefferson's Manual* and which in 1837 the House adopted as the authority "to govern the House in all cases to which they are applicable." The selection which follows is from Section LIII, entitled "Impeachment." It is re-printed in *Impeachment — Selected Materials*, 21-26.

SEC. LIII. — IMPEACHMENT.

603. Inception of Impeachment proceedings in the House.

In the House of Representatives there are various methods of setting an impeachment in motion: by charges made on the floor on the responsibility of a Member or Delegate (III, 2342, 2400, 2469, 2503)*; by charges preferred by a memorial, which is usually referred to a com-

* References of this nature are to *Hinds' Precedents*.

mittee for examination (III, 2364, 2491, 2494, 2406, 2409, 2515); by a message from the President (III, 2294, 2319); by charges transmitted from the legislature of a State (III, 2469) or Territory (III, 2487) or from a grand jury (III, 2488); or from facts developed and reported by an investigating committee of the House (III, 2399, 2444).

604. A proposition to Impeach a question of privilege.

A direct proposition to impeach is a question of high privilege in the House and at once supersedes business otherwise in order under the rules governing the order of business (III, 2045-2048). It may not even be superseded by an election case, which is also a matter of high privilege (III, 2581). It does not lose its privilege from the fact that a similar proposition has been made at a previous time during the same session of Congress (III, 2408), previous action of the House not affecting it (III, 2053). So, also, propositions relating to an impeachment already made are privileged (III, 2400, 2402, 2410); but a resolution simply proposing an investigation, even though impeachment may be a possible consequence, is not privileged (III, 2050, 2546). But where a resolution of investigation positively proposes impeachment or suggests that end, it has been admitted as of privilege (III, 2051, 2052, 2401, 2402).

605. Investigation of Impeachment charges.

The impeachment having been made on the floor by a Member (III, 2342, 2400), or charges suggesting impeachment having been made by memorial (III, 2495, 2520, 2516) or even appearing through common fame (III, 2385, 2506), the House has at times ordered an investigation at once. At other times it has refrained from ordering investigation until the charges had been examined by a committee (III, 2364, 2488, 2491, 2492, 2494, 2504, 2513).

606. Procedure of committee in Investigating.

The House has always examined the charges by its own committee before it has voted to impeach (III, 2294, 2487, 2501). This committee has sometimes been a select committee (III, 2342, 2487, 2494), sometimes a standing committee (III, 2400, 2409). In some instances the committee has made its inquiry ex parte (III, 2511, 2319, 2343, 2366, 2385, 2403, 2496); but in the later practice the sentiment of committees has been in favor of permitting the accused to explain, present witnesses, cross-examine

(III, 2445, 2471, 2518), and be represented by counsel (III, 2470, 2501, 2511, 2516).

607. Impeachment carried to the Senate.

Its committee on investigation having reported, the House may vote the impeachment (III, 2367, 2412), and, after having notified the Senate by message (III, 2413, 2446), may direct the impeachment to be presented at the bar of the Senate by a single Member (III, 2294), or by two (III, 2319, 2343, 2367), or even five Members (III, 2445). These Members in one notable case represented the majority party alone, but ordinarily include representation of the minority party (III, 2445, 2472, 2505). The chairman of the committee impeaches at the bar of the Senate by oral accusation (III, 2413, 2446, 2473), and requests that the Senate take order as to appearance; but in only one case has the parliamentary law as to sequestration and committal been followed (III, 2118, 2296), later inquiry resulting in the conclusion that the Senate had no power to take into custody the body of the accused (III, 2324, 2367). Having delivered the impeachment the committee return to the House and report verbally (III, 2413, 2446).

608. The writ of summons for appearance of respondent.

The managers for the House of Representatives attend in the Senate after the articles have been exhibited and demand that process issue for the attendance of respondent (III, 2451, 2478), after which they return and report verbally to the House (III, 2423, 2451). The Senate thereupon issue a writ of summons, fixing the day of return (III, 2423, 2451). . . .

Appendix B

Rules of the Senate for Impeachment Trials

Once an official is impeached by a majority vote of the House of Representatives, House Managers transmit this information to the Senate. The procedure in the Senate is prescribed by its rules. The following excerpt is from *Impeachment — Selected Materials*, 711-713.

Following are the major provisions of rules used by the Senate during impeachment trials. With the exception of Rule XI, which was adopted May 28, 1935, the rules have remained unchanged since their adoption March 2, 1868, for the trial of President Johnson.

I. Whensoever the Senate shall receive notice from the House of Representatives that managers are appointed on their part to conduct an impeachment against any person and are directed to carry articles of impeachment to the Senate, the Secretary of the Senate shall immediately inform the House of Representatives that the Senate is ready to receive the managers for the purpose of exhibiting such articles of impeachment, . . .

II. When the managers of an impeachment shall be introduced at the bar of the Senate and shall signify that they are ready to exhibit articles of impeachment against any person, the Presiding Officer of the Senate shall direct the Sergeant at Arms to make proclamation . . . after which the articles shall be exhibited, and then the Presiding Officer of the Senate shall inform the managers that the Senate will take proper order on the subject of the impeachment, of which due notice shall be given to the House of Representatives.

III. Upon such articles being presented to the Senate, the Senate shall, at 1 o'clock afternoon of the day (Sunday excepted) following such presentation, or sooner if ordered by the Senate, proceed to the consideration of such articles and shall continue in session from day to day (Sundays excepted) after the trial shall commence (unless otherwise ordered by the Senate) until final judgment shall be rendered, and so much longer as may, in its judgment, be needful. Before proceeding to the consideration of the articles of impeachment, the Presiding Officer shall administer the oath hereinafter provided to the members of the Senate then present and to the other members of the Senate as they shall appear, whose duty it shall be to take the same.

IV. When the President of the United States or the Vice President of the United States, upon whom the powers and duties of the office of President shall have devolved, shall be impeached, the Chief Justice of the Supreme Court of the United States shall preside; and in a case requiring the said Chief Justice to preside notice shall be given to him by the Presiding Officer of the Senate of the time and place fixed for the consideration of the articles of impeachment, as aforesaid, with a request to attend; and the said Chief Justice shall preside over the Senate during the consideration of said articles and upon the trial of the person impeached therein.

V. The Presiding Officer shall have power to make and issue, by himself or by the Secretary of the Senate, all orders, mandates, writs, and precepts authorized by these rules or by the Senate. . . .

VI. The Senate shall have power to compel the attendance of witnesses, to enforce obedience to its orders, mandates, writs, precepts, and judgments, to preserve order, and to punish in a summary way contempts of, and disobedience to, its authority, orders, mandates, writs, precepts, or judgments, and to make all lawful orders, rules, and regulations which it may deem essential or conductive to the ends of justice. . . .

VII. The Presiding Officer of the Senate shall direct all necessary preparations in the Senate Chamber, and the

Presiding Officer of the trial shall direct all the forms of proceedings while the Senate is sitting for the purpose of trying an impeachment, and all forms during the trial not otherwise specially provided for. And the Presiding Officer of the trial may rule all questions of evidence and incidental questions, which ruling shall stand as the judgment of the Senate, unless some member of the Senate shall ask that a formal vote be taken thereon, in which case it shall be submitted to the Senate for decision; or he may at his option, in the first instance, submit any such question to a vote of the members of the Senate. . . .

VIII. Upon the presentation of articles of impeachment and the organization of the Senate as herein before provided, a writ of summons shall issue to the accused, . . . If the accused, after service, shall fail to appear, either in person or by attorney, on the day so fixed therefor as aforesaid, or, appearing, shall fail to file his answer to such articles of impeachment, the trial shall proceed, nevertheless, as upon a plea of not guilty. If a plea of guilty shall be entered, judgment may be entered thereon without further proceedings.

IX. At 12:30 o'clock afternoon of the day appointed for the return of the summons against the person impeached, the legislative and executive business of the Senate shall be suspended, and the Secretary of the Senate shall administer an oath to the returning officer. . . . Which oath shall be entered at large on the records.

X. The person impeached shall then be called to appear and answer the articles of impeachment against him. If he appear, or any person for him, the appearance shall be recorded, stating particularly if by himself, or by agent or attorney, naming the person appearing and the capacity in which he appears. If he do not appear, either personally or by agent or attorney, the same shall be recorded.

XI. In the trial of any impeachment the Presiding Officer of the Senate, upon the order of the Senate, shall appoint a committee of twelve Senators to receive evidence and take testimony . . . Unless otherwise ordered by the Senate, the rules of procedure and practice in the Senate when sitting on impeachment trials shall govern the procedure and practice of the committee so appointed. . . . but nothing herein shall prevent the Senate from sending for any witness and hearing his testimony in open Senate, or by order of the Senate having the entire trial in open Senate.

XII. At 12:30 o'clock afternoon of the day appointed for the trial of an impeachment, the legislative and executive business of the Senate shall be suspended, and the Secretary shall give notice to the House of Representatives that the Senate is ready to proceed upon the impeachment of ————————— in the Senate Chamber, which chamber is prepared with accommodations for the reception of the House of Representatives.

XIII. The hour of the day at which the Senate shall sit upon the trial of an impeachment shall be (unless otherwise ordered) 12 o'clock m.; and when the hour for such thing shall arrive, the Presiding Officer of the Senate shall so announce; and thereupon the Presiding Officer upon such trial shall cause proclamation to be made, and the business of the trial shall proceed. The adjournment of the Senate sitting in said trial shall not operate as an adjournment of the Senate; but on such adjournment the Senate shall resume the consideration of its legislative and executive business.

XIV. The Secretary of the Senate shall record the proceedings in cases of impeachment as in the case of legislative proceedings, and the same shall be reported in the same manner as the legislative proceedings of the Senate.

XV. Counsel for the parties shall be admitted to appear and be heard upon an impeachment.

XVI. All motions made by the parties or their counsel shall be addressed to the Presiding Officer, and if he, or any Senator, shall require it, they shall be committed to writing, and read at the Secretary's table.

XVII. Witnesses shall be examined by one person on behalf of the party producing them, and then cross-examined by one person on the other side.

XVIII. If a Senator is called as a witness, he shall be sworn, and give his testimony standing in his place.

XIX. If a Senator wishes a question to be put to a witness, or to offer a motion or order (except a motion to adjourn), it shall be reduced to writing, and put by the Presiding Officer.

XX. At all times while the Senate is sitting upon the trial of an impeachment the doors of the Senate shall be kept open, unless the Senate shall direct the doors to be closed while deliberating upon its decisions.

XXI. All preliminary or interlocutory questions, and all motions, shall be argued for not exceeding one hour on each side, unless the Senate shall, by order, extend the time.

XXII. The case, on each side, shall be opened by one person. The final argument on the merits may be made by two persons on each side (unless otherwise ordered by the Senate upon application for that purpose), and the argument shall be opened and closed on the part of the House of Representatives.

XXIII. On the final question whether the impeachment is sustained, the yeas and nays shall be taken on each article of impeachment separately; and if the impeachment shall not, upon any of the articles presented, be sustained by the votes of two-thirds of the members present, a judgment of acquittal shall be entered; but if the person accused in such articles of impeachment shall be convicted upon any of said articles by the votes of two-thirds of the members present, the Senate shall proceed to pronounce judgment, and a certified copy of such judgment shall be deposited in the office of the Secretary of State.

XXIV. All the orders and decisions shall be made and had by yeas and nays, which shall be entered on the record, and without debate, subject, however, to the operation of Rule VII, except when the doors shall be closed for deliberation, and in that case no member shall speak more than once on one question, and for not more than ten minutes on an interlocutory question, and for not more than fifteen minutes on the final question, unless by consent of the Senate, to be had without debate, . . .

XXV. Witnesses shall be sworn. . . . Which oath shall be administered by the Secretary or any other duly authorized person. All process shall be served by the Sergeant at Arms of the Senate, unless otherwise ordered by the court.

XXVI. If the Senate shall at any time fail to sit for the consideration of articles of impeachment on the day or hour fixed therefor, the Senate may, by an order to be adopted without debate, fix a day and hour for resuming such consideration.

Appendix C

Articles of Impeachment
Against President Andrew Johnson

Andrew Johnson is the only President to have been impeached by the House and tried in the Senate. His case is, therefore, unique in American legal and constitutional annals. The reader can find the full transcript of the Senate trial in the three-volume *Trial of Andrew Johnson, President of the United States, Before the Senate of the United States, on Impeachment by the House of Representatives for High Crimes and Misdemeanors*, published by the Government Printing Office in 1868. Sections of these proceedings are re-printed in *Impeachment — Selected Materials*, 203-370. The following selection is the charges.

ARTICLE I

That said Andrew Johnson, President of the United States, on the 21st day of February, in the year of our Lord 1868, at Washington, in the District of Columbia, unmindful of the high duties of his office, of his oath of office, and of the requirement of the Constitution that he should take care that the laws be faithfully executed, did unlawfully, and in violation of the Constitution and laws of the United States, issue an order in writing for the removal of Edwin M. Stanton from the office of Secretary for the Department of War, said Edwin M. Stanton having been theretofore duly appointed and commissioned, by and with the advice and consent of the Senate of the United States, as such Secretary, and said Andrew Johnson, President of the United States, on the 12th day of August, in the year of our Lord 1867, and during the recess of said Senate, having suspended by his order Edwin M. Stanton from said office, and within twenty days after the first day of the next meeting of said Senate — that is to say, on the 12th day of December, in the year last aforesaid — having reported to said Senate such suspension, with the evidence and reasons for his action in the case and the name of the person designated to perform the duties of such office temporarily until the next meeting of the Senate, and said Senate thereafterwards, on the 13th day of January, in the year of our Lord 1868, having duly considered the evidence and reasons reported by said Andrew Johnson for said suspension, and having refused to concur in said suspension, whereby and by force of the provisions of an act entitled "An act regulating the tenure of certain civil offices," passed March 2, 1867, said Edwin M. Stanton did forthwith resume the functions of his office, whereof the said Andrew Johnson had then and there due notice, and said Edwin M. Stanton, by reason of the premises, on said 21st day of February, being lawfully entitled to hold said office of Secretary for the Department of War, which said order for the removal of said Edwin M. Stanton is, in substance, as follows, . . .

Which order was unlawfully issued with intent then and there to violate the act entitled "An act regulating the tenure of certain civil offices," passed March 2, 1867; and with the further intent, contrary to the provisions of said act, in violation thereof, and contrary to the provisions of the Constitution of the United States, and without the advice and consent of the Senate of the United States, the said Senate then and there being in session, to remove said Edwin M. Stanton from the office of Secretary for the Department of War, the said Edwin M. Stanton being then and there Secretary of War, and being then and there in the due and lawful execution and discharge of the duties of said office, whereby said Andrew Johnson, President of the United States, did then and there commit, and was guilty of a high misdemeanor in office.

ARTICLE II

That on said 21st day of February, in the year of our

Lord 1868, at Washington, in the District of Columbia, said Andrew Johnson, President of the United States, unmindful of the high duties of his office, of his oath of office, and in violation of the Constitution of the United States, and contrary to the provisions of an act entitled "An act regulating the tenure of certain civil offices," passed March 2, 1867, without the advice and consent of the Senate of the United States, said Senate then and there being in session, and without authority of law, did, with intent to violate the Constitution of the United States and the act aforesaid, issue and deliver to one Lorenzo Thomas a letter of authority, in substance as follows, . . .

Then and there being no vacancy in said office of Secretary for the Department of War, whereby said Andrew Johnson, President of the United States, did then and there commit, and was guilty of a high misdemeanor in office.

ARTICLE III

That said Andrew Johnson, President of the United States, on the 21st day of February, in the year of our Lord 1868, at Washington, in the District of Columbia, did commit and was guilty of a high misdemeanor in office in this, that without authority of law, while the Senate of the United States was then and there in session, he did appoint one Lorenzo Thomas to be Secretary for the Department of War ad interim, without the advice and consent of the Senate and with intent to violate the Constitution of the United States, no vacancy having happened in said office of Secretary for the Department of War during the recess of the Senate, and no vacancy existing in said office at the time, . . .

ARTICLE IV

That said Andrew Johnson, President of the United States, unmindful of the high duties of his office and of his oath of office, in violation of the Constitution and laws of the United States, on the 21st day of February, in the year of our Lord 1868, at Washington, in the District of Columbia, did unlawfully conspire with one Lorenzo Thomas, and with other persons to the House of Representatives unknown, with intent, by intimidation and threats, unlawfully to hinder and prevent Edwin M. Stanton, then and there the Secretary for the Department of War, duly appointed under the laws of the United States, from holding said office of Secretary for the Department of War, contrary to and in violation of the Constitution of the United States and of the provisions of an act entitled "An act to define and punish certain conspiracies," approved July 31, 1861, whereby said Andrew Johnson, President of the United States, did then and there commit, and was guilty of a high crime in office.

ARTICLE V

That said Andrew Johnson, President of the United States, unmindful of the high duties of his office and of his oath of office, on the 21st day of February, in the year of our Lord 1868, and on divers other days and times in said year, before the 2d day of March, A.D. 1868, at Washington, in the District of Columbia, did unlawfully conspire with one Lorenzo Thomas, and with other persons to the House of Representatives unknown, to prevent and hinder the execution of an act entitled "An act regulating the tenure of certain civil offices," passed March 2, 1867, and in pursuance of said conspiracy did unlawfully attempt to prevent Edwin M. Stanton, then and there being Secretary for the Department of War, duly appointed and commissioned under the laws of the United States, from holding said office, whereby the said Andrew Johnson, President of the United States, did then and there commit and was guilty of a high misdemeanor in office.

ARTICLE VI

That said Andrew Johnson, President of the United States, unmindful of the high duties of his office and of his oath of office, on the 21st day of February, in the year of our Lord 1868, at Washington, in the District of Columbia, did unlawfully conspire with one Lorenzo Thomas, by force to seize, take, and possess the property of the United States in the Department of War, and then and there in the custody and charge of Edwin M. Stanton, Secretary for said Department, contrary to the provisions of an act entitled "An act to define and punish certain conspiracies," approved July 31, 1861, and with intent to violate and disregard an act entitled "An act regulating the tenure of certain civil offices," passed March 2, 1867, whereby said

Andrew Johnson, President of the United States, did then and there commit a high crime in office.

ARTICLE VII

That said Andrew Johnson, President of the United States, unmindful of the high duties of his office and of his oath of office, on the 21st day of February, in the year of our Lord 1868, at Washington, in the District of Columbia, did unlawfully conspire with one Lorenzo Thomas with intent unlawfully to seize, take, and possess the property of the United States in the Department of War, in the custody and charge of Edwin M. Stanton, Secretary for said Department, with intent to violate and disregard the act entitled "An act regulating the tenure of certain civil offices," passed March 2, 1867, whereby said Andrew Johnson, President of the United States, did then and there commit a high misdemeanor in office.

ARTICLE VIII

That said Andrew Johnson, President of the United States, unmindful of the high duties of his office and of his oath of office, with intent unlawfully to control the disbursements of the moneys appropriated for the military service and for the Department of War, on the 21st day of February, in the year of our Lord 1868, at Washington, in the District of Columbia, did unlawfully and contrary to the provisions of an act entitled "An act regulating the tenure of certain civil offices," passed March 2, 1867, and in violation of the Constitution of the United States, and without the advice and consent of the Senate of the United States, and while the Senate was then and there in session, there being no vacancy in the office of Secretary for the Department of War, with intent to violate and disregard the act aforesaid, then and there issue and deliver to one Lorenzo Thomas a letter of authority in writing, in substance as follows, . . . whereby said Andrew Johnson, President of the United States, did then and there commit and was guilty of a high misdemeanor in office.

ARTICLE IX

That said Andrew Johnson, President of the United States, on the 22d day of February, in the year of our Lord 1868, at Washington, in the District of Columbia, in disregard of the Constitution and the laws of the United States, duly enacted, as Commander in Chief of the Army of the United States, did bring before himself then and there William H. Emory, a major-general by brevet in the Army of the United States, actually in command of the Department of Washington and the military forces thereof, and did then and there, as such Commander in Chief, declare to and instruct said Emory that part of a law of the United States, passed March 2, 1867, entitled "An act making appropriations for the support of the Army for the year ending June 30, 1868, and for other purposes," especially the second section thereof which provides among other things, that "all orders and instructions relating to military operations issued by the President or Secretary of War shall be issued through the General of the Army, and, in case of his inability, through the next in rank," was unconstitutional and in contravention of the commission of said Emory, and which said provision of law had been theretofore duly and legally promulgated by general order for the government and direction of the Army of the United States, as the said Andrew Johnson then and there well knew, with intent thereby to induce said Emory, in his official capacity as commander of the Department of Washington, to violate the provisions of said act, and to take and receive, act upon, and obey such orders as he, the said Andrew Johnson, might make and give, and which should not be issued through the General of the Army of the United States, according to the provisions of said act, and with the further intent thereby to enable him, the said Andrew Johnson, to prevent the execution of an act entitled "An act regulating the tenure of certain civil offices," passed March 2, 1867, and to unlawfully prevent Edwin M. Stanton, then being Secretary for the Department of War, from holding said office and discharging the duties thereof, whereby said Andrew Johnson, President of the United States, did then and there commit and was guilty of a high misdemeanor in office.

ARTICLE X

That said Andrew Johnson, President of the United States, unmindful of the high duties of his office and the dignity and proprieties thereof, and of the harmony and courtesies which ought to exist and be maintained between the executive and legislative branches of the Government of the United States, designing and intending to set aside the rightful authority and powers of Congress, did attempt to bring into disgrace, ridicule, hatred, contempt, and reproach the Congress of the United States and the several branches thereof, to impair and destroy the regard and respect of all the good people of the United States for the Congress and legislative power thereof (which all officers of the Government ought inviolably to preserve and maintain), and to excite the odium and resentment of all the good people of the United States against Congress and the laws by it duly and constitutionally enacted, and in pursuance of his said design and intent, openly and publicly, and before divers assemblages of the citizens of the United States convened in divers parts thereof to meet and receive said Andrew Johnson as the Chief Magistrate of the United States, did, on the 18th day of August, in the year of our Lord 1866, and on divers other days and times, as well before as afterwards, make and deliver with a loud voice certain intemperate, inflammatory, and scandalous harangues, and did therein utter loud threats and bitter menaces as well against Congress as the laws of the United States duly enacted thereby, amid the cries, jeers, and laughter of the multitudes then assembled and within hearing, which are set forth in the several specifications hereinafter written, in substance and effect, that is to say:

Specification first. — In this, that at Washington, in the District of Columbia, in the Executive Mansion, to a committee of citizens who called upon the President of the United States, speaking of and concerning the Congress of the United States, said Andrew Johnson, President of the United States, heretofore, to wit, on the 18th day of August, in the year of our Lord 1866, did, in a loud voice, declare in substance and effect, among other things, that is to say:

"So far as the executive department of the Government is concerned, the effort has been made to restore the Union, to heal the breach, to pour oil into the wounds which were consequent upon the struggle, and (to speak in common phrase) to prepare, as the learned and wise physician would, a plaster healing in character and coextensive with the wound. We thought, and we think, that we had partially succeeded; but as the work progresses, as reconstruction seemed to be taking place and the country was becoming reunited, we found a distrubing and marring element opposing us. . . .

"We have witnessed in one department of the Government every endeavor to prevent the restoration of peace, harmony, and union. We have seen hanging upon the verge of the Government, as it were, a body called, or which assumes to be, the Congress of the United States, while in fact it is a Congress of only a part of the States. We have seen this Congress pretend to be for the Union when its every step and act tended to perpetrate disunion and make a disruption of the States inevitable. . . . We have seen Congress gradually encroach step by step upon constitutional rights and violate, day after day and month after month, fundamental principles of the Government. We have seen a Congress that seemed to forget that there was a limit to the sphere and scope of legislation. We have seen a Congress in a minority assume to exercise power which, allowed to be consummated, would result in despotism or monarchy itself."

Specification second. — In this, that at Cleveland, in the State of Ohio, heretofore, to wit, on the 3d day of September, in the year of our Lord 1866, before a public assemblage of citizens and others, said Andrew Johnson, President of the United States, speaking of and concerning the Congress of the United States did, in a loud voice, declare in substance and effect among other things, that is to say:

"I will tell you what I did do. I called upon your Congress that is trying to break up the Government. . . .

"In conclusion, beside that, Congress had taken much pains to poison their constituents against him. But what had Congress done? Have they done anything to restore the union of these States? No; on the contrary, they had done everything to prevent it; . . . But Congress, factious and domineering, had undertaken to poison the minds of the American people."

Specification third. — In this, that at St. Louis, in the State of Missouri, heretofore, to wit, on the 8th day of September, in the year of our Lord 1866, before a public assemblage of citizens and others, said Andrew Johnson, President of the United States, speaking of and concerning the Congress of the United States, did, in a loud voice, declare, in substance and effect, among other things, that is to say:

"Go on. Perhaps if you had a word or two on the subject of New Orleans you might understand more about it than you do. And if you will go back — if you will go back and ascertain the cause of the riot at New Orleans, perhaps you will not be so prompt in calling out 'New Orleans.' If you will take up the riot at New Orleans and trace it back to its source or its immediate cause, you will find out who was responsible for the blood that was shed there. If you will take up the riot at New Orleans and trace it back to the Radical Congress, you will find that the riot at New Orleans was substantially planned. If you will take up the pro-ceedings in their caucuses, you will understand that they there knew that a convention was to be called which was extinct by its power having expired; that it was said that the intention was that a new government was to be organized, and on the organization of that government the intention was to enfranchise one portion of the population, called the colored population, who had just been eman-cipated, and at the same time disenfranchise white men. When you design to talk about New Orleans you ought to understand what you are talking about. . . . I will tell you a few wholesome things that have been done by this Radical Congress in connection with New Orleans and the extension of the elective franchise. . . .

"I know that I have been traduced and abused. I know it has come in advance of me here, as elsewhere, that I have attempted to exercise an arbitrary power in resisting laws that were intended to be forced upon the Government; that I had exercised that power; that I had abandoned the party that elected me, and that I was a traitor because I exercised the veto power . . . yes, that I was a traitor. And I have been traduced. I have been slandered. I have been maligned. I have been called Judas Iscariot, and all that. Now, my countrymen here tonight, it is very easy to indulge in epithets; it is easy to call a man a Judas and cry out traitor; but when he is called upon to give arguments and facts it is very easy to indulge in epithets; it is easy to call a man a Judas and he was one of the twelve apostles. Oh yes: the twelve apostles had a Christ. The twelve apostles had a Christ, and he never could have had a Judas unless he had had twelve apostles. If I have played the Judas, who has been my Christ that I have played the Judas with? Was it Thad Stevens? Was it Wendell Philips? Was it Charles Sumner? These are the men that stop and compare themselves with the Saviour; and everybody that differs with them in opinion, and to try and stay and arrest the diabolical and nefarious policy, is to be denounced as a Judas. . . .

"Well, let me say to you, if you will stand by me in this action; if you will stand by me in trying to give the people a fair chance, soldiers and citizens, to participate in these offices, God being willing, I will kick them out. I will kick them out just as fast as I can.

"Let me say to you, in concluding, that what I have said I intended to say. I was not provoked into this, and I care not for their menaces, the taunts, and the jeers. I care not for threats. I do not intend to be bullied by my enemies nor overawed by my friends. But, God willing, with your help I will veto their measures whenever any of them come to me."

Which said utterances, declarations, threats, and harangues, highly censurable in any, are peculiarly indecent and unbecoming in the Chief Magistrate of the United States, by means whereof said Andrew Johnson has brought the high office of the President of the United States into contempt, ridicule, and disgrace, to the great scandal of all good citizens, whereby said Andrew Johnson, President of the United States, did commit, and was then and there guilty of, a high misdemeanor in office.

ARTICLE XI

That said Andrew Johnson, President of the United States, unmindful of the high duties of his office and of his oath of office, and in disregard of the Constitution and laws of the United States, did heretofore, to wit, on the 18th day of August, 1866, at the city of Washington, in the District of Columbia, by public speech, declare and affirm, in substance, that the Thirty-ninth Congress of the United States was not a Congress of the United States authorized by the Constitution to exercise legislative power under the same; but, on the contrary, was a Congress of only part of the States, thereby denying and intending to deny that the legislation of said Congress was valid or obligatory upon him, the said Andrew Johnson, except in so far as he saw fit to approve the same, and also thereby denying and intending to deny the power of the said Thirty-ninth Congress to propose amendments to the Constitution of the United States; and in pursuance of said declaration, the said Andrew Johnson, President of the United States, afterwards, to wit, on the 21st day of February, 1868, at the city of Washington, in the District of Columbia, did unlawfully and in disregard of the requirements of the Constitution, that he should take care that the laws be faithfully executed, attempt to prevent the execution of an act entitled "An act regulating the tenure of certain civil offices," passed March 2, 1867, by unlawfully devising and contriving, and attempting to devise and contrive, means by which he should prevent Edwin M. Stanton from forthwith resuming the functions of the office of Secretary for the Department of War, notwithstanding the refusal of the Senate to concur in the suspension theretofore made by said Andrew Johnson, of said Edwin M. Stanton from said office of Secretary for the Department of War, and also by further unlawfully devising and contriving, and attempting to devise and contrive, means then and there to prevent the execution of an act entitled "An act making appropriations for the support of the Army for the fiscal year ending June 30, 1868, and for other purposes," approved March 2, 1867, and also to prevent the execution of an act entitled "An act to provide for the more efficient government of the rebel States," passed March 2, 1867; whereby the said Andrew Johnson, President of the United States, did then, to wit, on the 21st day of February, 1868, at the city of Washington, commit and was guilty of a high misdemeanor in office.

And the House of Representatives, by protestation, saving to themselves the liberty of exhibiting at any time hereafter any further articles or other accusation or impeachment against the said Andrew Johnson, President of the United States, and also of replying to his answers which he shall make unto the articles herein preferred against him, and of offering proof to the same and every part thereof, and to all and every other article, accusation, or impeachment which shall be exhibited by them, as the case shall require, do demand that the said Andrew Johnson may be put to answer the high crimes and misdemeanors in office herein charged against him, and that such proceedings, examinations, trials, and judgments may be thereupon had and given as may be agreeable to law and justice.

SCHUYLER COLFAX
Speaker of the House of Representatives

Appendix D

HOUSE COMMITTEE ON THE JUDICIARY
93rd CONGRESS

Peter W. Rodino, Jr., New Jersey, *Chairman*

Democrats
Harold D. Donohue, Massachusetts
Jack Brooks, Texas
Robert W. Kastenmeier, Wisconsin
Don Edwards, California
William L. Hungate, Missouri
John Conyers, Jr., Michigan
Joshua Eilberg, Pennsylvania
Jerome R. Waldie, California
Walter Flowers, Alabama
James R. Mann, South Carolina
Paul S. Sarbanes, Maryland
John F. Seiberling, Ohio
George E. Danielson, California
Robert F. Drinan, Massachusetts
Charles B. Rangel, New York
Barbara Jordan, Texas
Ray Thornton, Arkansas
Elizabeth Holtzman, New York
Wayne Owens, Utah
Edward Mezvinsky, Iowa

Republicans
Edward Hutchinson, Michigan
Robert McClory, Illinois
Henry P. Smith III, New York
Charles W. Sandman, Jr., New Jersey
Tom Railsback, Illinois
Charles E. Wiggins, California
David W. Dennis, Indiana
Hamilton Fish, Jr., New York
Wiley Mayne, Iowa
Lawrence J. Hogan, Maryland
William J. Keating, Ohio
M. Caldwell Butler, Virginia
William S. Cohen, Maine
Trent Lott, Mississippi
Harold V. Froehlich, Wisconsin
Carlos J. Moorhead, California
Joseph J. Maraziti, New Jersey

Bibliographical Overview

Unfortunately impeachment is neglected too much in the critical literature; indeed, there is no satisfactory study of impeachment in the United States. Any review of the bibliography must begin with Raoul Berger, *Impeachment: The Constitutional Problems* (Cambridge, 1973). It is the most scholarly study available, yet it does not adequately deal with the history of impeachment in America. Its strength lies in its historical development of precedents in England as well as legal and historical analyses of some impeachable offenses, especially treason and "good behavior" of judges. The chapter on "high crimes and misdemeanors" is extremely well done; it is a re-working of Berger's article "Impeachment for 'High Crimes and Misdemeanors'" which appeared originally in the *Southern California Law Review*, XLIV (1971). Berger deals with the Chase and Johnson cases, but refers to the others only as they relate to the legal principles he is analyzing. As a lawyer, Berger stresses the role of the courts in limiting executive encroachments; fearing excessive political partisanship, he prefers the remedy of impeachment only as a measure of last resort. Anyone wishing to delve further into the English precedents and into some detailed analyses will find Berger's book invaluable. His bibliography is also excellent, but the researcher will have to view it only as a starting point, especially in the area of pre-Stuart English history.

The only recent work on the twelve American impeachments is Irving Brant's *Impeachment: Trials and Errors* (New York, 1972). Unfortunately it is very weak. Brant seems concerned primarily with condemning the attempt to impeach Justice William O. Douglas in 1970. He argues that impeachment was intended by the Framers of the Constitution as a remedy only against criminal violations, and he very narrowly rejects the many English and American precedents which do not conform to this thesis. In spite of Brant's earlier scholarly successes, especially his biographical studies of James Madison, his book is poorly reasoned and cannot be acceptable as a valid history of American impeachments and trials. An older study by Alexander Simpson, *A Treatise of Federal Impeachments* (New York, 1916), is badly outdated and of little value.

Relatively few scholarly articles have been written on impeachment, and they are primarily legal analyses by lawyers and political scientists rather than historical studies on impeachment. Among the best are David Y. Thomas, "The Law of Impeachment in the United States," *American Political Science Review*, II (1908), which is obviously out-dated; Leon R. Yankwich, "Impeachment of Civil Officers Under the Federal Constitution," *Georgetown Law Journal*, XXVI (1938); and Paul S. Fenton, "The Scope of the Impeachment Power," *Northwestern University Law Review*, LXV (1970). Others include Lynn W. Turner, "The Impeachment of John Pickering," *American Historical Review*, LIV (1949); Richard B. Lillich, "The Chase Impeachment," *American Journal of Legal History*, IV (1960); Martha Ziskind, "Judicial Tenure in the American Constitution," *Supreme Court Review* (1969); and John

Feerick, "Impeaching Federal Judges: A Study of the Constitutional Provisions," *Fordham Law Review*, XXXIX (1970).

Only one of the twelve American impeachments and trials has been the subject of any extensive study, and that understandably is of President Andrew Johnson. But even that event has not been studied adequately. Until recently the only good monograph was David M. DeWitt's *The Impeachment and Trial of Andrew Johnson, Seventeenth President of the United States* (New York, 1903). Other accounts of the Johnson impeachment and trial have been included as small parts (sometimes only a few sentences or paragraphs) in histories of Reconstruction, constitutional histories, or biographies of Johnson or others associated with the event. Among the better works is Eric L. McKitrick, *Andrew Johnson and Reconstruction* (Chicago, 1960). Another good description, representing the traditional view of the impeachment and trial, is James G. Randall and David Donald, *Civil War and Reconstruction* (Lexington, Mass., 1969). The most recent monograph is Michael Les Benedict, *The Impeachment and Trial of Andrew Johnson* (New York, 1973). Benedict interprets the events of Reconstruction to justify the impeachment and removal of President Johnson. His book also contains a good recent bibliography on the Johnson impeachment and trial, including pertinent works on Reconstruction, President Andrew Johnson himself, and other prominent individuals of that period. The reader interested in the full transcript of the House impeachment and the Senate trial of President Johnson will find it in the three-volume *Trial of Andrew Johnson, President of the United States, Before the Senate of the United States, on Impeachment by the House of Representatives for High Crimes and Misdemeanors* (Washington, D.C., 1868).

Except for the Johnson case, little is to be found on the other impeachments and trials. An occasional brief mention is made of the Pickering or Chase cases, but rarely will one find any of the others even mentioned, whether in a general text, a constitutional history, or a legal history. Histories of the presidency, of the Congress, or of the courts are equally negligent. Nor are there adequate biographies of the impeached officials.

Because of the lack of secondary materials, one must go directly to the primary sources. The best are the discussions in the House and the Senate during the impeachments and the trials. They are found in the appropriately dated sections of the *Annals of Congress*, the *Congressional Globe* and the *Congressional Record*. Committee reports, too numerous to list here, also contain vital information, especially reports of the House Judiciary Committee and other investigatory committees. As indicated in the text of this book, the sections of *Hinds' Precedents of the House of Representatives* (Washington, D.C., 1907) and *Cannon's Precedents of the House of Representatives* (Washington, D.C., 1935), dealing with impeachment are invaluable. Already mentioned in the Preface but worth repeating is *Impeachment — Selected Materials*, House Committee Print, Committee on the Judiciary, House of Representatives, 93rd Congress, 1st Session, October, 1973 (Washington, D.C., 1973), which contains much background material provided for the members of the House Judiciary Committee.

In addition to the current materials excerpted in the text, representative recent publications valuable to understanding some of the controversial issues in the Nixon crisis include "Power of Impeachment" in Congressional Quarterly's *Guide to the Congress of the United States, 1971*; "Controversy Over the Presidential Impoundment of

Appropriated Funds," *The Congressional Digest*, LII (1973); and I. F. Stone, "Impeachment," *The New York Review of Books*, June 28, 1973.

As the controversy centering on President Richard M. Nixon develops, very important materials will be forthcoming. Reports submitted by counsel John M. Doar and Albert E. Jenner on behalf of the House Judiciary Committee and by James D. St. Clair on behalf of the White House should provide up-dates on what constitutes an impeachable offense to augment both *Hinds' Precedents* and *Cannon's Precedents*. They undoubtedly will contribute largely to decisions by Congressmen and by the general public relative to impeachment. Indeed, one might hope that out of this constitutional crisis will emerge a body of literature that will erase the misconceptions and misunderstandings about impeachment and impeachability, so they will no longer be an American dilemma.

Index